Jane Bull

Get Set, Sew

The beginner's sewing machine book

DK | Penguin Random House

DESIGN AND TEXT Jane Bull
PHOTOGRAPHER Andy Crawford
PROJECT EDITOR Kathryn Meeker
US EDITOR Margaret Parrish
DESIGNER Charlotte Bull
MANAGING EDITOR Penny Smith
SENIOR MANAGING ART EDITOR Marianne Markham
JACKET DESIGNER Amy Keast
PRE-PRODUCTION CONTROLLER Andy Hilliard
PRODUCTION CONTROLLER Che Creasey
CREATIVE TECHNICAL SUPPORT Sonia Charbonnier
CATEGORY PUBLISHER Mary Ling

First American Edition, 2015
Published in the United States by DK Publishing
345 Hudson Street, New York, New York 10014

Copyright © 2015 Dorling Kindersley Limited
A Penguin Random House Company
Copyright © 2015 Jane Bull
15 16 17 18 19 10 9 8 7 6 5 4 3 2 1
001—270922—July/2015

A catalog record for this book is available
from the Library of Congress.
ISBN: 978-1-4654-3587-3

DK books are available at special discounts when purchased in
bulk for sales promotions, premiums, fund-raising, or
educational use. For details, contact: DK Publishing Special
Markets, 345 Hudson Street, New York, New York 10014
Special Sales@dk.com.

Printed and bound in China
All images © Dorling Kindersley Limited
For further information see: www.dkimages.com

A WORLD OF IDEAS:
SEE ALL THERE IS TO KNOW
www.dk.com

This book
is for my mother,
Barbara Owen,
who, like her sewing
machine, is always
on the go.

Contents

10 Getting Started

- Get to know your sewing machine • How stitches work
- Threading a machine • How to fill a bobbin • Ready to sew
- Now, for a test drive! • Sewing tips and problem solving

25 Sewing Essentials

- Sewing essentials • Fabrics • Trims and things

33 Helpful Skills

- Hand sewing • How to join fabric • How to make
paper templates • Make a SOFT HEART project

45 Get Set, Sew!

46 • 5 ways to use a dish towel: Tote bag, Wrap'n'roll,
Apron, Dust cover, and Shoe bag

58 • Goodie bags

60 • Make it easy pillows

68 • Bobtail rabbits

74 • Flutterbys

78 • Handy bags

82 • Square Peg and friends

94 • Pin watch

96 • Garlands

98 • Floppy pots

102 • Playful pups

106 • Wacky ornaments

108 • Zip it!

112 • 3-D chickens

114 • Sleep well, Ted

118 • Monster invasion

122 • Templates • Index • Acknowledgments

Let's start your sewing machine!

Getting Started

Get to know your sewing machine • Go for a test drive • Gather your sewing essentials • Learn helpful skills • *Make a soft heart* project

Get to know your Sewing Machine

Find out what all the different features on your machine do. Machines come in many styles, but they all work in a similar way. Use the manual that comes with your machine to help you recognize the parts.

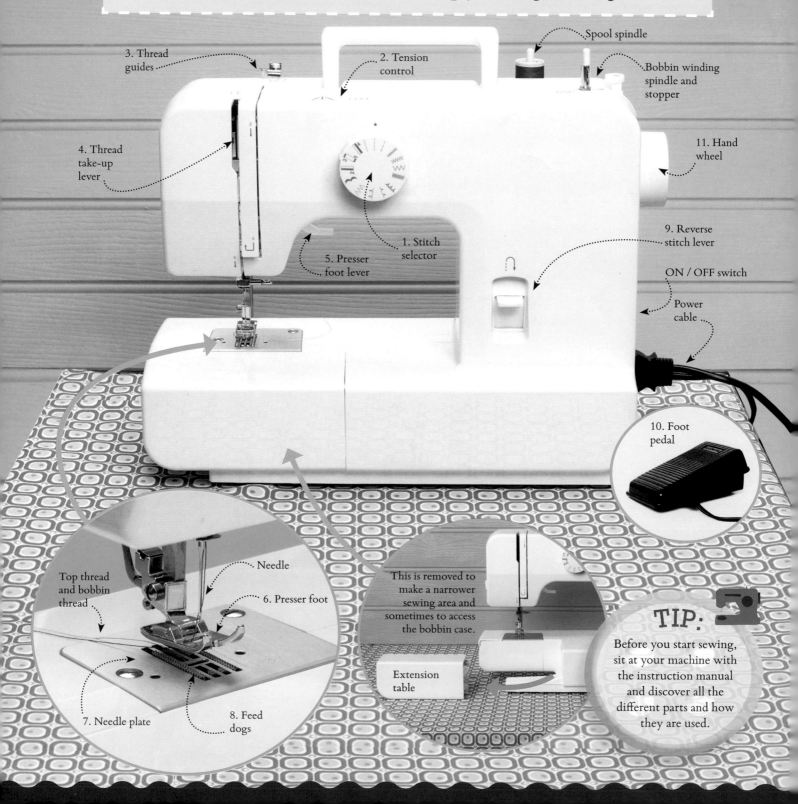

Spool spindle

3. Thread guides

2. Tension control

Bobbin winding spindle and stopper

4. Thread take-up lever

11. Hand wheel

1. Stitch selector

9. Reverse stitch lever

5. Presser foot lever

ON / OFF switch

Power cable

10. Foot pedal

Top thread and bobbin thread

Needle

6. Presser foot

This is removed to make a narrower sewing area and sometimes to access the bobbin case.

7. Needle plate

8. Feed dogs

Extension table

TIP:

Before you start sewing, sit at your machine with the instruction manual and discover all the different parts and how they are used.

What the parts do...

1. STITCH SELECTOR: This controls the stitch style and length. Some machines, however, have a separate dial for the stitch length.

2. TENSION CONTROL: This controls how loose or tight the thread is while you're sewing.

3. THREAD GUIDES: These show the direction the thread goes to get to the needle. They also control the movement of the thread. Refer to your manual on how to thread your machine.

4. THREAD TAKE-UP LEVER: This moves up and down while the needle is stitching to help control the flow of the thread.

5. PRESSER FOOT LEVER: This lever raises and lowers the presser foot. Lift it up to insert and remove fabric and put it down to hold the fabric when sewing.

6. PRESSER FOOT: The foot holds the fabric in place and works with the feed dogs to move the fabric along while it's being stitched. There are different types of feet for different jobs. The all-purpose foot shown here is used for all the projects that follow.

7. NEEDLE PLATE: This is a metal plate under the presser foot that holds the feed dogs. It is where the bobbin thread comes up to meet the needle coming down. There are lines in the metal to use as guides for different seam widths.

8. FEED DOGS: These rough teeth work up and down to move the fabric gently through the machine while you stitch.

9. REVERSE STITCH LEVER: If you hold this down the machine will stitch backward. When the lever is released, the machine will stitch forward again.

10. FOOT PEDAL: This sits on the floor. It drives the motor when you press down on it with your foot. It acts like an accelerator in a car, allowing you to control the speed.

11. HAND WHEEL: Use the hand wheel when you need to move the needle up and down manually. Turn the wheel toward you. It also spins around when the motor is running.

12. BOBBIN CASE: This holds the small spool of bottom thread. Some machines have it at the top and others at the side. See more about bobbins on pages 16-17.

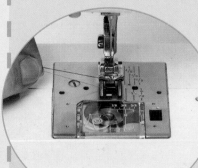

12. TOP LOAD bobbin case   12. SIDE LOAD bobbin case

Choosing a sewing machine

• **KEEP IT SIMPLE:** As a beginner, you don't need a machine that's complicated and has lots of functions. But you definitely shouldn't buy a toy machine either.

• **PRICE:** Look for a good brand and do some research. You don't need to spend too much money.

• **INSTRUCTION MANUAL:** A new machine will come with an instruction manual. If it's a second-hand machine and does not have a manual, go online to find information.

Sewing safety

• **NOT A TOY:** Remember that your machine is not a plaything; it is a tool. Always use it sensibly and carefully.

• **POWER OFF:** Always turn the power off when threading a needle or when doing any other task that doesn't require power.

• **SIT DOWN:** Don't try sewing while standing up.

• **WATCH YOUR FINGERS:** Keep your hands and fingertips away from the needle when sewing.

• **NO SPEEDING:** Learn to control your speed using the foot pedal. Practice sewing with scrap fabric before you begin. If in doubt, take your foot off the pedal and STOP.

How stitches work

A sewing machine uses two threads to make a stitch, unlike hand stitching, which uses only one. It has a top thread on a large spool and a lower thread on a small spool called a bobbin.

Top thread

This is a large spool of thread. Use this thread to fill your bobbin so you have matching stitches.

Bobbin

These small spools are empty when purchased. You will need to fill them with thread to match your fabric.

Which thread goes where

When the machine is running, the two threads wind together to make a row of stitches. The top thread shows on top of the work and the bobbin thread shows at the back of the work. The stitches should all look even. If you're not sure about your stitches, check with your instruction book.

Top thread

Fabric

Bobbin thread

How a stitch is made

These diagrams show how the needle comes down through the fabric, into the bobbin case, and picks up the bobbin thread to form a stitch. The sequence is repeated again and again.

Needle

Fabric

Bobbin

Stitch selector

Simply move the dial around to select the stitch style. Some machines have a separate dial for selecting the length of the stitches, too, but this model has it all in one. ALWAYS remember to lift the needle out of the fabric before turning the dial.

Straight stitch

This is the only stitch you will need to make your sewing projects.

Zigzag stitch

Stitches like this can add decorative touches to your work. Zigzag stitch can also be used along the edge of a fabric to stop it from fraying.

Threading a machine

Threading your machine correctly is an essential first step to sewing. You will need to thread both the top and the bobbin threads.

NOTE: Turn off the power when threading the machine.

1 Place the spool of thread on the spindle.

2 Follow the arrows and thread guides.

3 Loop the thread through the thread take-up lever.

The top thread

Place the spool on the spindle, then follow the arrows, looping and winding the thread through the thread guides down to the needle. Check your machine manual for instructions.

NOTE: The needle and presser foot should be raised.

Use the hand wheel to raise the needle and the thread take-up lever.

4 Place the thread behind the thread hook.

5 Thread the needle from the front to the back, or as your machine requires.

6 Take the thread under the presser foot and out toward the back.

How to fill a bobbin

Each type of machine will have a different arrangement for filling a bobbin, but the principle is usually the same. Here is an example of how a typical bobbin is filled. Always use the bobbins provided with your machine, or buy extras of the same style and material, since they can vary in size depending on the brand.

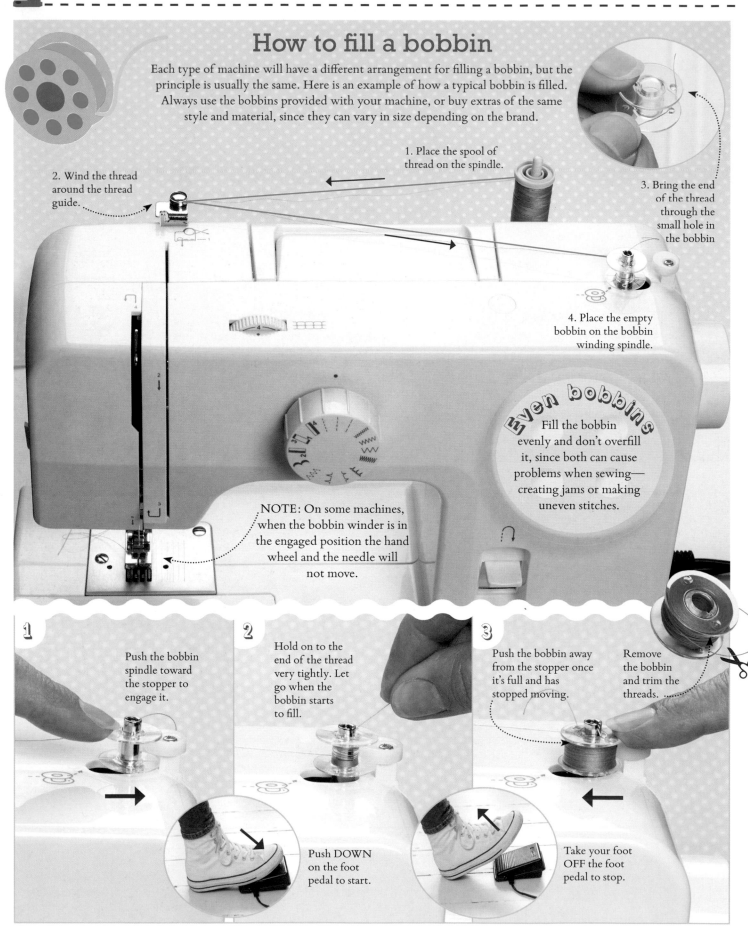

1. Place the spool of thread on the spindle.

2. Wind the thread around the thread guide.

3. Bring the end of the thread through the small hole in the bobbin

4. Place the empty bobbin on the bobbin winding spindle.

Even bobbins
Fill the bobbin evenly and don't overfill it, since both can cause problems when sewing—creating jams or making uneven stitches.

NOTE: On some machines, when the bobbin winder is in the engaged position the hand wheel and the needle will not move.

1 Push the bobbin spindle toward the stopper to engage it.

2 Hold on to the end of the thread very tightly. Let go when the bobbin starts to fill.

Push DOWN on the foot pedal to start.

3 Push the bobbin away from the stopper once it's full and has stopped moving.

Remove the bobbin and trim the threads.

Take your foot OFF the foot pedal to stop.

How to side load a bobbin
Some machines have a special holder for the bobbin that's placed into the side.

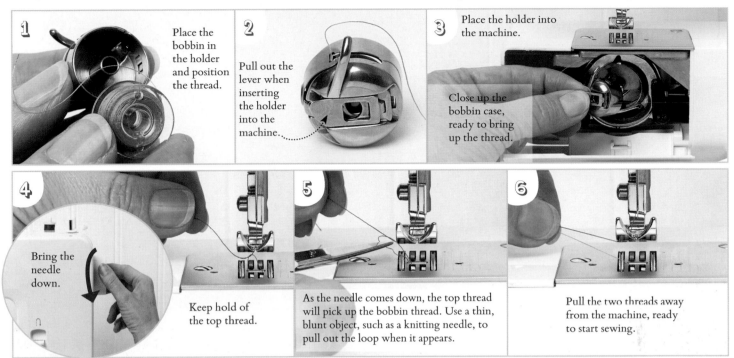

1 Place the bobbin in the holder and position the thread.

2 Pull out the lever when inserting the holder into the machine.

3 Place the holder into the machine.
Close up the bobbin case, ready to bring up the thread.

4 Bring the needle down.
Keep hold of the top thread.

5 As the needle comes down, the top thread will pick up the bobbin thread. Use a thin, blunt object, such as a knitting needle, to pull out the loop when it appears.

6 Pull the two threads away from the machine, ready to start sewing.

How to top load a bobbin
The bobbin can be placed straight into the machine.

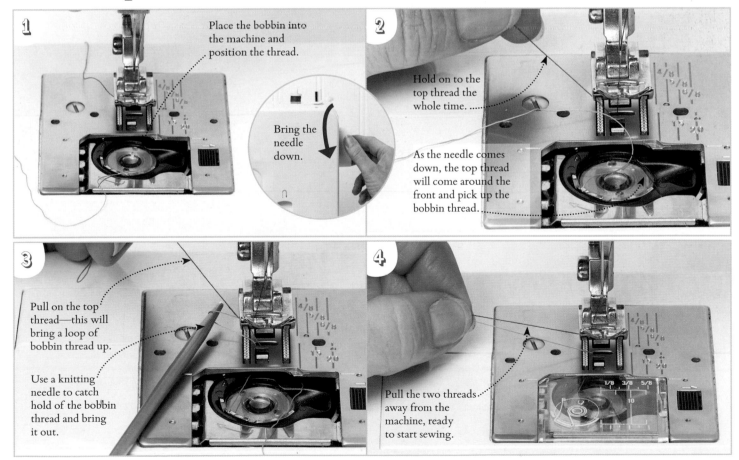

1 Place the bobbin into the machine and position the thread.
Bring the needle down.

2 Hold on to the top thread the whole time.
As the needle comes down, the top thread will come around the front and pick up the bobbin thread.

3 Pull on the top thread—this will bring a loop of bobbin thread up.
Use a knitting needle to catch hold of the bobbin thread and bring it out.

4 Pull the two threads away from the machine, ready to start sewing.

Ready to Sew

Your machine is set up, so now you're ready to start sewing. These basics will equip you with the skills to make the projects that follow. Learn how to start and stop sewing, straight stitch, reverse stitch, and how to turn corners. Then, go for a test drive.

Checklist
before you start...

1. Sewing machine plugged in and switched on.

2. Needle and bobbin threaded correctly.

3. Stitch type selected and all materials on hand.

4. Top and bobbin threads long enough to begin sewing.

5. Sitting correctly.

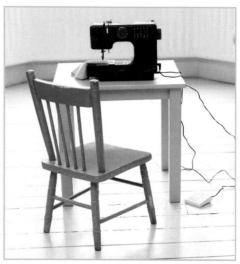

Sitting position

Place your machine on a firm work surface. Make sure you are sitting comfortably and that the machine is at the right height for you. Place the foot pedal where you can easily reach it.

Hand position

Place your hands in a triangular shape AWAY FROM THE NEEDLE.

Stop sewing
and remove work

• Take your foot away from the pedal so the machine won't start accidentally.
• Always raise the needle out of the fabric using the hand wheel, otherwise the needle might break when you remove the fabric.
• Cut the thread close to the fabric to leave a long length coming out of the machine—otherwise, you'll be rethreading constantly.

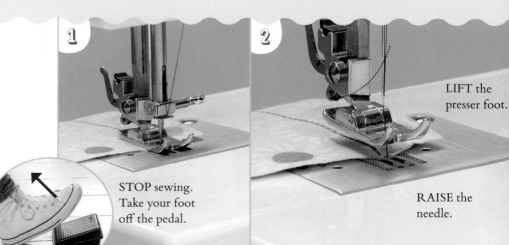

1 STOP sewing. Take your foot off the pedal.

2 LIFT the presser foot.

RAISE the needle.

Start sewing

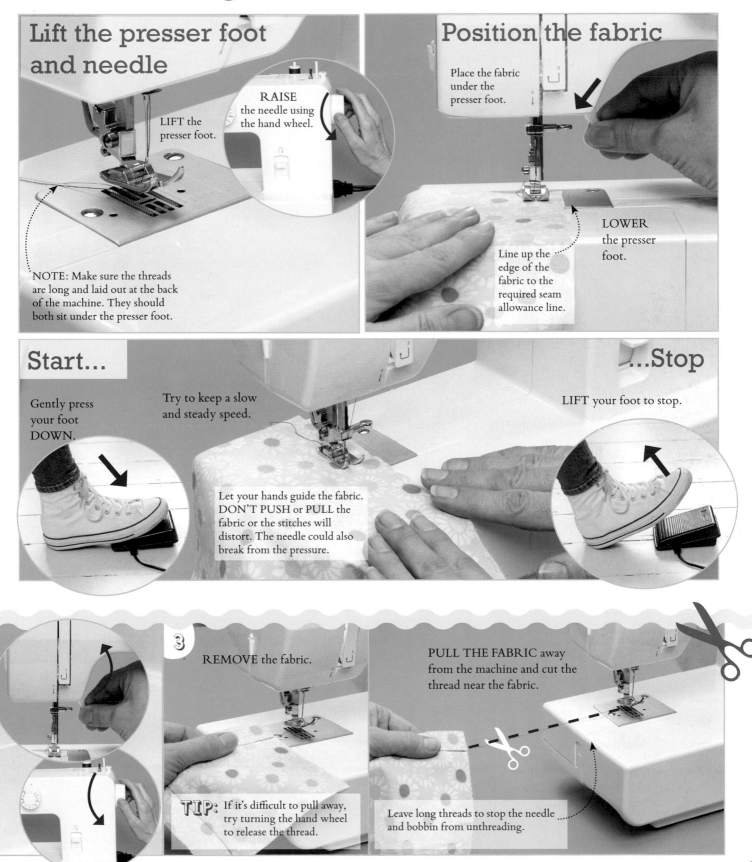

Lift the presser foot and needle

LIFT the presser foot.

RAISE the needle using the hand wheel.

NOTE: Make sure the threads are long and laid out at the back of the machine. They should both sit under the presser foot.

Position the fabric

Place the fabric under the presser foot.

LOWER the presser foot.

Line up the edge of the fabric to the required seam allowance line.

Start...

Gently press your foot DOWN.

Try to keep a slow and steady speed.

Let your hands guide the fabric. DON'T PUSH or PULL the fabric or the stitches will distort. The needle could also break from the pressure.

...Stop

LIFT your foot to stop.

③

REMOVE the fabric.

TIP: If it's difficult to pull away, try turning the hand wheel to release the thread.

PULL THE FABRIC away from the machine and cut the thread near the fabric.

Leave long threads to stop the needle and bobbin from unthreading.

Straight stitch

This is the basic machine stitch that's used for almost everything. Keeping a straight line can take some practice, so follow the tips shown here.

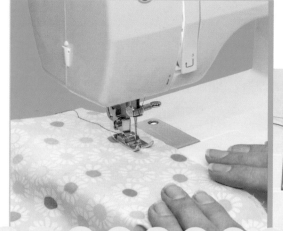

TIPS: How to keep a straight line

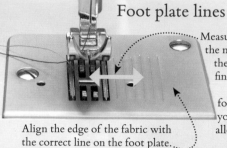

Foot plate lines

Measure from the needle to the lines to find which one to follow for your seam allowance.

Align the edge of the fabric with the correct line on the foot plate.

Reverse stitch

This stitch, also called lock stitch, is used at the beginning and end of a seam to stop the stitches from coming undone.

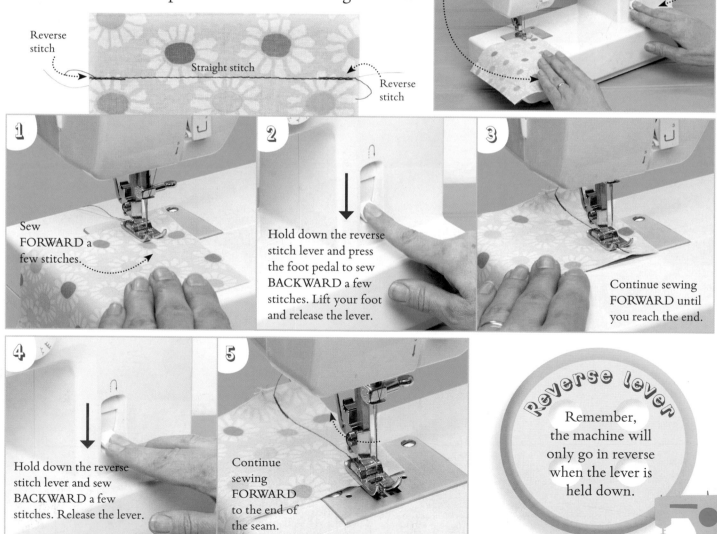

Reverse stitch

Straight stitch

Reverse stitch

Hold the fabric steady with your left hand.

Push down the reverse stitch lever with your right hand.

1 Sew FORWARD a few stitches.

2 Hold down the reverse stitch lever and press the foot pedal to sew BACKWARD a few stitches. Lift your foot and release the lever.

3 Continue sewing FORWARD until you reach the end.

4 Hold down the reverse stitch lever and sew BACKWARD a few stitches. Release the lever.

5 Continue sewing FORWARD to the end of the seam.

Reverse lever
Remember, the machine will only go in reverse when the lever is held down.

Practice sewing on striped fabric

Make a tape guide line

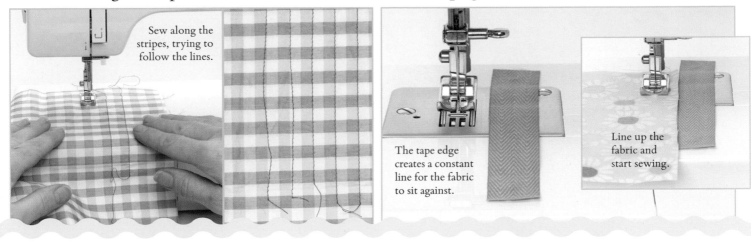

Sew along the stripes, trying to follow the lines.

The tape edge creates a constant line for the fabric to sit against.

Line up the fabric and start sewing.

Corners

This method is used when a sharp corner is needed. It doesn't have to be a right angle (as shown here). It's made by leaving the needle in the fabric, allowing you to PIVOT, or turn, the fabric around the needle.

Keep the needle in the fabric and pivot the fabric around it.

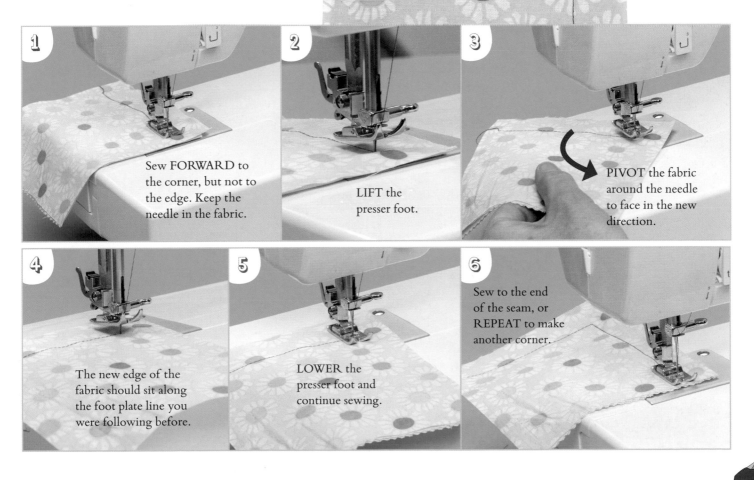

1 Sew FORWARD to the corner, but not to the edge. Keep the needle in the fabric.

2 LIFT the presser foot.

3 PIVOT the fabric around the needle to face in the new direction.

4 The new edge of the fabric should sit along the foot plate line you were following before.

5 LOWER the presser foot and continue sewing.

6 Sew to the end of the seam, or REPEAT to make another corner.

Now, for a test drive!

Go for a drive!

Use the skills you've learned so far to try out your machine.

TIP: Don't pull or push the fabric as you sew—guide it around gently. Needles can break if they're pulled.

You will need

- Scraps of cotton fabric
- Sewing essentials (pages 27–32)

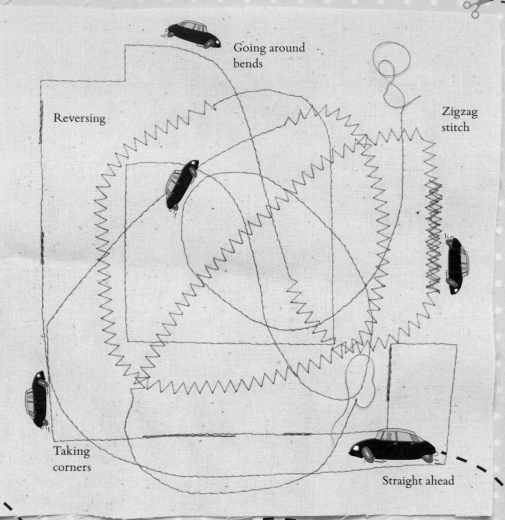

Going around bends

Reversing

Zigzag stitch

Taking corners

Straight ahead

Starting off...

1. Switch on your machine and make sure it is threaded properly.
2. Lift the needle and the presser foot.
3. Place the fabric in position.
4. Lower the presser foot.
5. Position your hands on the fabric, ready to sew.
6. Put your foot on the foot pedal to begin sewing.

⚠ Watch your speed

Press down gently on the foot pedal. Slowly move off.

TAKE YOUR FOOT OFF THE PEDAL TO STOP THE MACHINE.

Remember that it's not a race!

Turning a corner

1. Sew straight, then stop.
2. Make sure the needle is still in the fabric.
3. Lift the presser foot.
4. Move the fabric to face in the new direction.
5. Lower the presser foot and continue sewing.

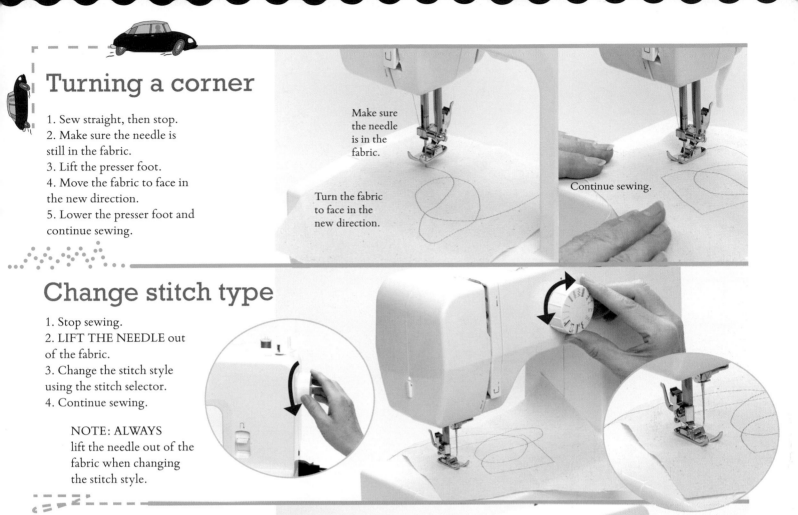

Make sure the needle is in the fabric.

Turn the fabric to face in the new direction.

Continue sewing.

Change stitch type

1. Stop sewing.
2. LIFT THE NEEDLE out of the fabric.
3. Change the stitch style using the stitch selector.
4. Continue sewing.

NOTE: ALWAYS lift the needle out of the fabric when changing the stitch style.

Reverse stitch

1. Stop sewing FORWARD.
2. Press down the reverse lever.
3. At the same time, guide the fabric with your other hand.
4. Start sewing BACKWARD.
5. Release the lever and continue sewing FORWARD.

NOTE: The machine will only go in reverse while you press the lever down.

Gently hold on to the fabric as you reverse.

Press down the reverse stitch lever.

Finish and remove the fabric

1. Stop sewing, and take your foot off the pedal.
2. Lift the presser foot.
3. Lift the needle out of the fabric using the hand wheel.
4. Gently pull the fabric away from under the machine.
5. Snip the threads close to the fabric, not the machine.

Sewing tips & problem solving

It's no fun when your machine decides not to work. Here are simple tips for avoiding problems and solutions for fixing some of the most common problems.

Power off

When something needs to be fixed, always follow these steps.
1. Take your foot off the pedal and stop sewing.
2. Switch off the power.
3. Take a moment to try to figure out what's wrong.
4. Check with your instruction manual for more help.

Avoid problems

• **KEEPING THE NEEDLE THREADED:** Remember not to cut the needle and bobbin threads too short. If the threads aren't long enough, they will pull back as you start and the machine will need to be rethreaded.

• **DON'T PULL OR PUSH THE FABRIC:** Use your hands to guide the fabric under the presser foot. Pulling and pushing will make uneven stitches and can cause the needle to break.

• **RAISE THE NEEDLE AND PRESSER FOOT:** Always do this when removing fabric, changing stitch style, and threading the needle. If the needle is left in the fabric it will break.

• **CORRECT THREADING:** Make sure the threads are looped around all the hooks and levers and the thread goes through the needle the right way.

• **BE PREPARED:** Check that you've prepared the fabric as instructed in the step-by-step instructions and positioned it under the presser foot so that you have enough room for the seam allowance.

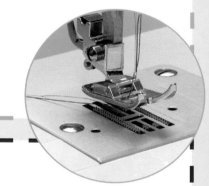

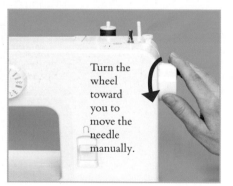

Turn the wheel toward you to move the needle manually.

Turning the hand wheel
The hand wheel is mainly used for raising the needle so you can place or remove fabric from under the presser foot. It's also useful if...
• you want to move work slowly under the presser foot, ready to start sewing.
• after sewing, the fabric doesn't want to come away from the machine easily. Turn the hand wheel slightly to move the feed dogs and release the threads underneath.

Solve problems

With any problem it's best to refer to the advice in your machine's instruction manual.

• **STITCHING LOOKS WRONG:** This is usually when the top thread and bobbin thread are not working together properly. For example, if there are loops showing from the stitching below, or on top, the stitch tension needs to be adjusted.

• **FABRIC JAMMED IN THE MACHINE:** After turning off the machine, lift the presser foot and use the hand wheel to raise the needle.

You will need to cut away the threads under the fabric that are caught in the feed dogs. Remove the bobbin (and case) and clean out the area under the needle plate. You may need to remove it to do this. Check your instruction manual for help.

• **BROKEN NEEDLE:** This can happen when you accidentally sew over a pin or forget to take the needle out of the fabric. Also, make sure you are using the correct needle for your machine and fabric.

In addition to your sewing machine, you will need...

Sewing Essentials

Have these ready for every project—sewing kit, scissors, ruler, pens, pencil, chalk, thread, fabric, and notions.

Don't forget your pincushion

Sewing Essentials

Every project will need a sewing kit and other equipment, such as scissors for cutting fabric. Gather what you will need and keep all items on hand.

Sewing Kit
for hand sewing

Safety pins

Sewing needles

Small, sharp scissors

Needle threader

Sewing thread in different colors

Seam ripper

Tape measure

Dressmaking pins

Thimble

The following pages show more essential equipment and materials used throughout the book.

You will need

All the projects begin with a list of the materials and equipment you will need. The Sewing essentials are listed each time.

More sewing essentials

Ruler

In addition to a flexible tape measure, it's good to keep a ruler on hand. The longer the better, so you can measure large pieces of fabric and make templates.

Remember!
Measure twice, cut once

Measurements

In this book, sizes are given in inches and centimeters—use one or the other, but don't mix them up. Making templates (see page 38) explains how to cut out large pieces of fabric using a ruler and triangle.

Scissors

Use your scissors for the job they are designed for. Do not use your fabric scissors when cutting paper—this will dull them.

Large sharp scissors for fabric

Paper scissors

Pencil

Felt-tip permanent marker

Chalk

Making marks

Pens: Use these for making templates.
Chalk: Use chalk to make marks directly onto fabric. Ordinary chalk will work, or you can buy tailor's chalk from the craft store.

Pinking shears

These scissors have specially shaped blades that make a zigzag shape when they cut. Use them to give a decorative finish to projects (see Goodie bags, page 58) and to keep edges of fabric from fraying at seams.

Zigzag blades

Iron

Some projects work better if the fabric seams are flattened. TAKE CARE! Use the iron on an ironing board and hold it correctly. Irons get hot and the steam can scald you.

ASK FOR HELP!

Bobbins

Also known as spools, these hold the thread that makes the back of the stitch. Some will come with the machine, but buy more of the same size. Fill up a few bobbins and keep them on hand.

Threads

There a number of types of thread available, but an all-purpose type of thread will work well. Have a selection of colors to go with your fabric and to fill up the extra bobbins to match.

Sewing machine

Your sewing machine will come with a set of tools for cleaning it and supecial equipment, such as needles and different presser feet. It's good to get extra bobbins to fill with different colored thread, too.

Fabrics

Get a feel for fabric. Fabric comes in many forms, from the softest silk to stiff canvas. But, to keep it simple, here is all you need to know to make some great projects.

Cotton

This is a lightweight fabric that is often used to make dresses and shirts. It comes in different designs and patterns, which makes it ideal for craft work.

Fraying edges

Cotton is a woven fabric, which means it's made from threads crossing over one another. When the fabric is cut, threads will come loose and cause fraying. Use pinking shears to help prevent this.

Different colored threads create a striped design

White cotton printed with a red design

Where to find fabric

Fabric is readily available in craft stores and at markets. It's sold by the length in yards or meters and comes in different widths. You can usually buy as much by length as you need. Useful small amounts of fabric called fat quarters are sold for patchwork. Alternatively, you can recycle fabric, using clothes you no longer need.

Fabric with a multicolored print design

White fabric printed in orange to create a spotted design

Solid colors

Woven check design is called gingham

Muslin is always a cream color

Felt

Felt is a very useful fabric. The best thing about it is that it doesn't fray like cotton. Because it's quite thick and soft, it can be tricky to sew on a machine. It's perfect, however, for adding decoration to projects.

Muslin

A very versatile and inexpensive fabric, muslin is good to use for practice projects. It's thicker than most cotton fabrics so it makes a good backing to give cotton some weight—like the Floppy pots on page 98.

Getting to know your fabric

It's helpful to understand the names of the different parts of your fabric. These words will be mentioned in the step-by-step instructions.

Raw edge, where the fabric has been cut. It is likely to fray.

The selvage runs along the width of the fabric. It won't fray.

Right side showing

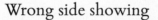

Wrong side

Wrong side showing

Right side

Right or wrong side

Printed cotton fabric has a very distinctive right and wrong side. The right side shows up darker and the pattern is more defined. With solid-colored cottons there is often no right or wrong side.

Wrong sides facing

This means that the backs of the pieces of fabric (the wrong sides) are touching each other. The Goodie bags project shown here does this. The right sides stay showing all the time as you sew around the edges.

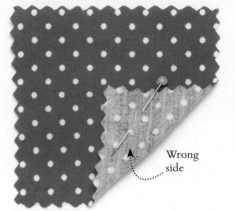

The stitches show on the outside.

Goodie bags, page 58

Right sides facing

It's more likely that the instructions will tell you to put the fronts of the fabrics (the right sides) together. This is so that once the project has been sewn it can be turned right side out to reveal the patterned sides of the fabric. The stitches will be hidden inside.

Sewing will be done on the wrong side of the fabric.

The stitches are now inside.

Bobtails, page 68

Right sides are lying face to face.

Trims and things

Buttons

Use buttons to add decoration.

Bright and pretty ribbons and buttons can really transform a project into something special that's individual to you. Ready-made cotton twill tapes can save time and add a nice finishing touch.

Ribbons and trims

With these, the possibilities are endless. They really do come in all colors, shapes, and sizes. Use them as edgings, like on the pillows on page 64, or make them a feature, as on page 117.

Ribbon

Narrow rickrack

Pom-pom tape

Large rickrack

Recycling

Keep leftover scraps of ribbon and save ribbons that come with gifts and flowers. They will all come in handy.

This is a woven cotton tape that can be used a number of ways, as shown with the bag handles on page 48 or Flutterbys on page 76.

Cotton tape

Hook and loop tape, such as Velcro®, is used as a fastening. See the Pin watch on page 94.

Hook and loop tape

Soft-toy filling

This is often used for projects in this book. This is a supersoft polyester fiber that is lightweight and washable. It is sold in most craft stores.

Binding tape

This comes ready-folded and designed for making a neat edge to fabric. It is used for Bunting on page 77.

More know-how to help with
the projects coming up.

Helpful Skills

Included: Hand sewing, How to join
fabric, How to make paper templates,
and *Make a soft heart* project

Hand sewing

Not all sewing can be done on a sewing machine. Some jobs, such as finishing and sewing on buttons, have to be done by hand.

Sewing needles

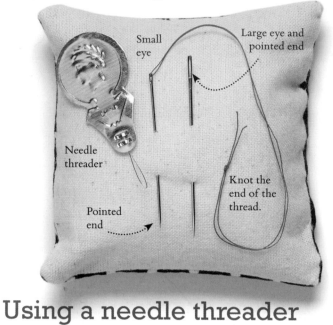

Small eye

Large eye and pointed end

Needle threader

Pointed end

Knot the end of the thread.

Threading a needle

Cut the end of the thread with sharp scissors.

Push the thread through the eye of the needle.

How long do I cut thread?

If you work with thread that is too long it will become tangled and slow you down. Cut a piece roughly the length of your fingers to your elbow.

Cut thread about as long as this line

Using a needle threader

1

1. Push the threader through the eye of the needle.

2. Put the end of the thread though the wire loop.

2

Pull the wire loop and thread back through the eye.

3

Remove the needle threader.

Sewing stitches

All stitches have a different job to do. Some finish a project and others add decoration.

How to start and finish

Always begin sewing with a knot at the end of your thread to keep it in place. To end a row of stitches, make a tiny stitch, but do not pull the thread tight. Bring the thread back up through the loop of the stitch and then pull it tight. Do this once more in the same spot to make a strong knot. Cut the thread.

Running stitch

This stitch can be used for joining fabric and adding decoration. It is similar to basting stitch (page 36).

Keep the stitches and the spaces between them small and even.

Whipstitch

These are tiny, neat, and even stitches that are almost invisible. Use them to top sew two finished edges together.

Insert the needle diagonally through the edge of the fabric from the back.

Slip stitch

Slip stitch is designed to join two folded edges, such as openings. It is used in projects like Bobtails (page 71) and Square Peg (page 91).

Slide the needle into the fold of the fabric.

Bring the needle out, then slide it into the opposite folded edge.

Sewing on a button

1

Secure the thread at the back of the fabric. Then put the button onto the needle and drop it down the thread.

2

Push the needle back through the opposite hole in the button.

3

Continue sewing up and down through the buttonholes and fabric.

4

1. To secure the button, bring the needle and thread up under the button.

2. Sew backward and forward behind the button. Cut the thread.

How to join fabric

What is a seam? A seam is the where two pieces are fabric are joined together with stitches, usually near the fabric edges. The space between the edge and the line of stitches is called the seam allowance.

Pinning fabric together

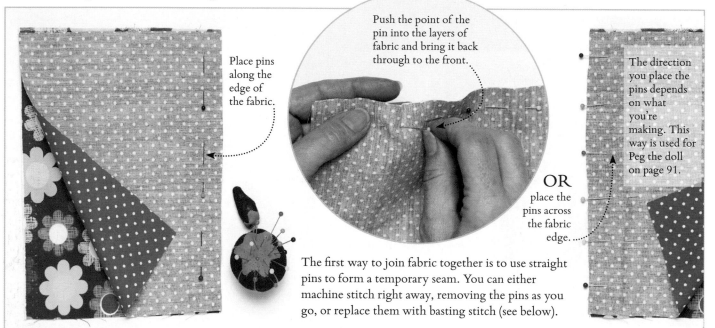

Place pins along the edge of the fabric.

Push the point of the pin into the layers of fabric and bring it back through to the front.

OR place the pins across the fabric edge.

The direction you place the pins depends on what you're making. This way is used for Peg the doll on page 91.

The first way to join fabric together is to use straight pins to form a temporary seam. You can either machine stitch right away, removing the pins as you go, or replace them with basting stitch (see below).

Basting stitch (basting)

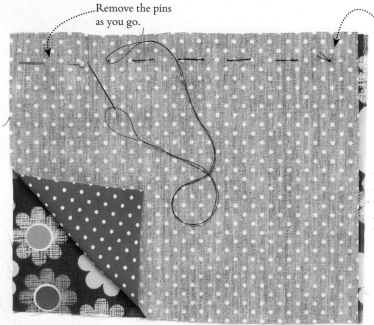

Remove the pins as you go.

Knot the thread.

Use thread that is a very diffrent color from your fabric.

Basting is a temporary stitch that holds a seam or trim in place until it's machine stitched. Basting stitches are removed after they've done their job.

When you reach the end, cut off the thread. Do not knot it. This makes it easier to remove later.

Sewing a seam

Begin machine stitching the seam, reverse stitch, then work along the edge of the fabric over the basting stitches. Reverse stitch when you reach the end of the seam.

Sew the same distance from the edge of the fabric the whole time—this space is called the seam allowance.

Removing basting

Take hold of the knot and pull on it to drag the thread out of the fabric.

NOTE: The thread may get stuck where it has been sewn over. If so, cut the basting thread and remove the pieces.

Opening out a seam

Flatten out the seam when you need the fabric to look like one piece.

Open up the seam and press it flat.

BE CAREFUL, IRONS ARE HOT! Ask an adult for help.

Unpicking a seam

Use a seam ripper to unpick the stitches along the seam.

Hook the sharp end under the stitch and draw it along the blade to cut the thread.

Pull the fabric apart as you go.

Wrong side

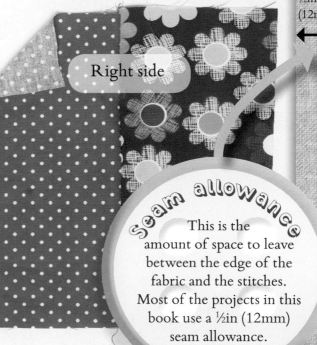

Right side

½in (12mm)

seam allowance
This is the amount of space to leave between the edge of the fabric and the stitches. Most of the projects in this book use a ½in (12mm) seam allowance.

How to make paper templates

Most of the projects in this book require paper templates. Here are some ways to help you cut the template to the size and shape you need.

You will need

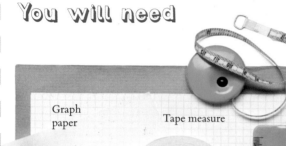

Graph paper

Tape measure

Tracing paper

Masking tape

Felt-tip pen

Paper scissors

Triangle

Large sheet of paper, such as brown paper or newspaper

Ruler

Square shape

Here's a quick way to make a square shape. Measure and mark the size your square needs to be along two perpendicular outer edges. Then, fold the corner of the paper toward the middle at those two marks. Cut along the edges.

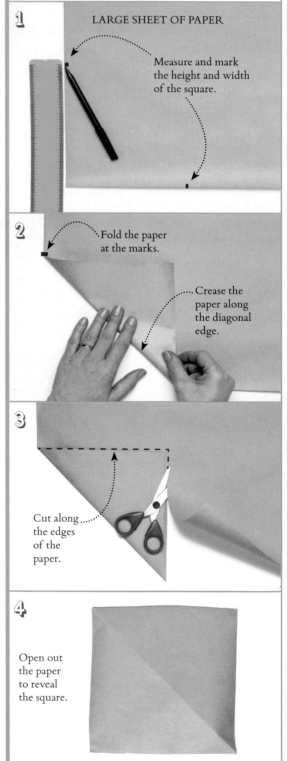

1 LARGE SHEET OF PAPER

Measure and mark the height and width of the square.

2 Fold the paper at the marks.

Crease the paper along the diagonal edge.

3 Cut along the edges of the paper.

4 Open out the paper to reveal the square.

Rectangular shape

When you need to cut a rectangular-shaped template, measure the height and width of the rectangle along the edges of the paper. Use the triangle to draw a vertical line.

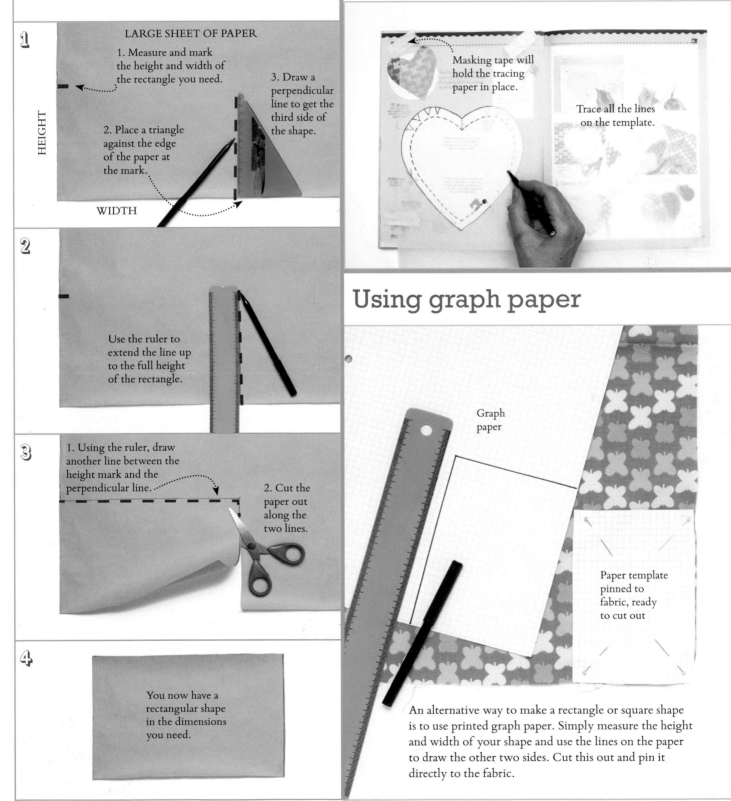

1

LARGE SHEET OF PAPER

1. Measure and mark the height and width of the rectangle you need.

3. Draw a perpendicular line to get the third side of the shape.

2. Place a triangle against the edge of the paper at the mark.

HEIGHT

WIDTH

2

Use the ruler to extend the line up to the full height of the rectangle.

3

1. Using the ruler, draw another line between the height mark and the perpendicular line.

2. Cut the paper out along the two lines.

4

You now have a rectangular shape in the dimensions you need.

Tracing templates

Some projects will have templates printed on the pages. These are shown life-sized and can be traced directly from the page onto tracing paper. This template can then be pinned to the fabric.

Masking tape will hold the tracing paper in place.

Trace all the lines on the template.

Using graph paper

Graph paper

Paper template pinned to fabric, ready to cut out

An alternative way to make a rectangle or square shape is to use printed graph paper. Simply measure the height and width of your shape and use the lines on the paper to draw the other two sides. Cut this out and pin it directly to the fabric.

Make a soft heart

You'll love this project. Step-by-step, it will introduce you to the skills and techniques you need to make all of the projects in the book.

Using a template

"V" shapes
After sewing the two shapes together, snip along these lines—it will help shape the fabric.

After sewing the fabric together, cut along the dotted line.

Templates will give you the size and shape of your pieces of fabric. The lines tell you where to cut the fabric and where to sew.

How to change the size

To make a project in a larger or smaller size simply scan the page on a copier and increase or decrease it to the size you want. Use the copy as your paper template and pin it directly to the fabric.

Solid line
Cut fabric out along this line.

Dotted line
Sew along this line.

The space between the two lines is the seam allowance—½in (12mm).

After sewing the fabric together, cut along dotted lines.

START sewing here

STOP sewing here

Opening
Sew up to these dots, leaving an opening so that you can fill the heart.

1 Make the paper template

Tape the tracing paper over the template on the page of the book.

Trace over all the lines.

Cut out the paper shape.

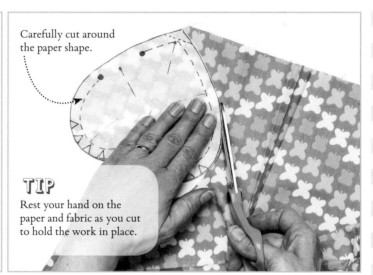

2 Pin to fabric and cut out

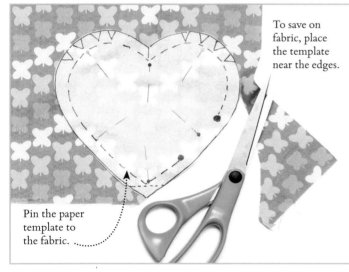

To save on fabric, place the template near the edges.

Pin the paper template to the fabric.

Carefully cut around the paper shape.

TIP

Rest your hand on the paper and fabric as you cut to hold the work in place.

3 Transfer the marks

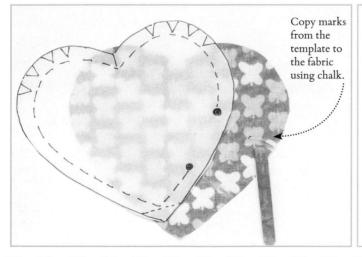

Copy marks from the template to the fabric using chalk.

4 Pin fabrics together

Pin the two pieces of fabric together.

Make sure the right sides are facing.

5 Sew the seam

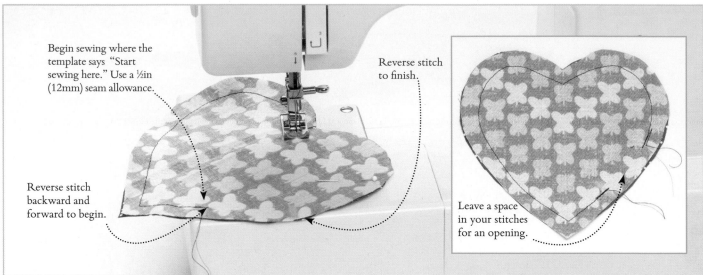

Begin sewing where the template says "Start sewing here." Use a ½in (12mm) seam allowance.

Reverse stitch to finish.

Reverse stitch backward and forward to begin.

Leave a space in your stitches for an opening.

6 Reducing bulk

Cut into the seam allowance as shown on the template.

Cut V notches around the curved edges.

Cut off the point, but be careful not to cut the stitches.

Cutting Tip

Why cut off corners and snip notches into the fabric? Cutting away some of the fabric around the seam will keep it from being too bulky when you turn it right side out. Be careful not to snip into the seam or it will create a hole.

7 Turning right sides out

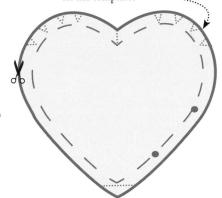

Bring the right side out, working it through the opening.

You will need

Knitting needle

Any blunt-ended tool such as this, or a pencil, will help you work into the corners.

Soft-toy filling

Soft-toy filling is a polyester fiber ideal for craft projects. It can be purchased from most craft stores.

8 Make a good shape

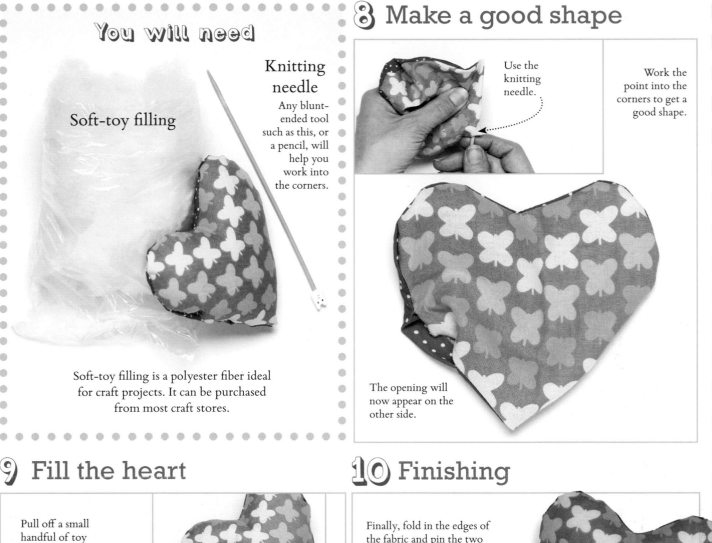

Use the knitting needle.

Work the point into the corners to get a good shape.

The opening will now appear on the other side.

9 Fill the heart

Pull off a small handful of toy filling and start pushing it through the opening.

Push the filling into all the parts of the shape, making sure it is evenly distributed.

10 Finishing

Finally, fold in the edges of the fabric and pin the two sides together.

Use slip stitch to sew the edges together (page 35).

Colorful ideas to try your sewing skills.

Get Set, Sew!

An array of projects • Dish towel transformations • Bags and pots to stow your stuff • Cheery streamers, bunting, and garlands • Lovable rabbits, pups, and more

5 ways to use a dish towel

Forget drying dishes! Pick up a dish towel and transform it into something different in just a few simple steps.

①

②

Lots of things to make

③

1 dish towel	=

What's so great about dish towels?
They are ready-to-use pieces of cotton cloth. No measuring is needed, and you don't have to worry about fraying edges. They come in all kinds of colors and designs. Don't confine them to the kitchen—make something special!

④

⑤

No.1
Tote bag

Make a bag in no time!
Fold a dish towel in half,
add some handles, sew up
the sides, and you have a bag.
What could be simpler?
It's the perfect tote for a
trip to the beach.

You will need

- Dish towel
- 2 strips cotton tape, 21in (53cm) long
- Sewing essentials (pages 27–32)

1

1. Find the center by folding the towel in half lengthwise.

2. Mark the center with the chalk.

3. Mark the center at the other end of the fold too.

2

1. Place each end of the tape 4½in (12cm) from the center line.

2. Baste the tape in place, making sure it is not twisted.

Secure the tape in place. Sew across the ribbon and down its sides.

3

Attach the tape to both ends of the towel.

Sewing across the tape in an "X" shape will help to secure it further.

4

1. Fold the towel in half with right sides facing.

Match the edges carefully.

2. Pin, baste, then sew the side edges together. Turn the bag right side out.

Tip for sewing the seam

Place the presser foot against the side of the hemmed edge of the dish towel to help guide your seam line.

No.2 Wrap'n'roll

You will need

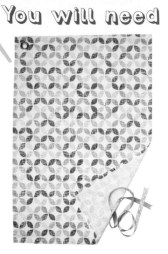

- Dish towel • Ribbon 41in (104cm) long • Sewing essentials (pages 27–32)

Portable pens

You can create a neat solution for storing all your equipment. Simply make folds in a dish towel and sew lines for pockets. The wrap is easy to carry, too.

1

1. Lay the cloth right-side down.

2. Fold the bottom of the dish towel up 10in (25cm).

2

1. Fold the ribbon in half.

3. Fold the bottom of the first fold up again, high enough to cover the ribbon.

2. Place the folded end on top of the folded dish towel 1in (2.5cm) from the edge.

4. Pin the folded edges and then baste them together.

5. Also pin the pockets together to hold them in place.

3

1. Measure how wide you want to make your pockets so they'll be big enough to hold your things.

2. Draw chalk lines along the folds to mark where to stitch.

4

Sew along the chalk lines to create the pockets. Reverse stitch at both ends of the line.

Place your pens and pencils in the pockets.

Now you're ready to roll!

No.3
Apron

Need to cover up?
Here's an idea for a
speedy apron solution.
The shaping at the top
forms casings through
which you can thread
the cotton twill
tape. Just sew
two seams and
you're done.

You will need

- Dish towel
- 2yds (2m) cotton tape
- Sewing essentials (pages 27–32)

Make a casing

A casing is
a tunnel made from
fabric that is used to enclose
a drawstring or elastic. Here
it's used to hold the cotton
twill tape that makes the
apron strings.

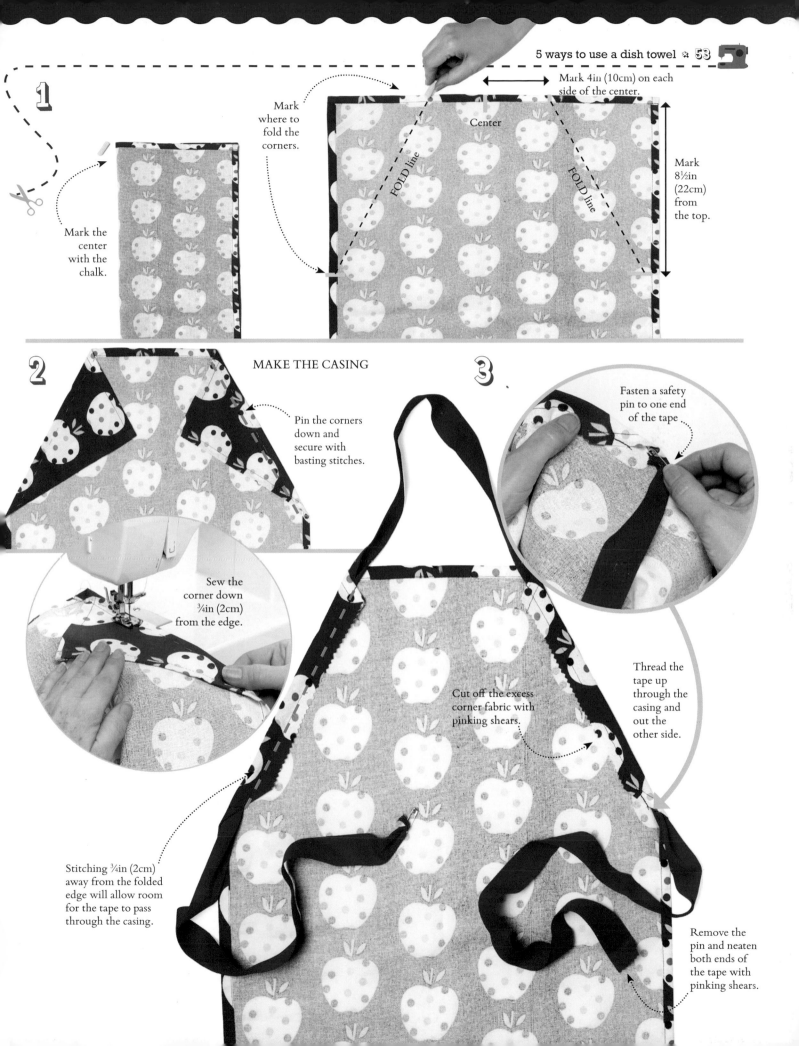

1

Mark the center with the chalk.

Mark where to fold the corners.

Mark 4in (10cm) on each side of the center.

Center

FOLD line

FOLD line

Mark 8½in (22cm) from the top.

2

Pin the corners down and secure with basting stitches.

MAKE THE CASING

Sew the corner down ¾in (2cm) from the edge.

3

Fasten a safety pin to one end of the tape

Thread the tape up through the casing and out the other side.

Cut off the excess corner fabric with pinking shears.

Stitching ¾in (2cm) away from the folded edge will allow room for the tape to pass through the casing.

Remove the pin and neaten both ends of the tape with pinking shears.

You will need

- Dish towel
- Sewing essentials (pages 27–32)

No.4 Dust cover

Make your sewing machine happy with this cute dust cover. It keeps the machine free from dust and the special pockets hold sewing essentials.

For a large machine

If you have a large sewing machine, a dish towel won't quite cover it. Try leaving the sides open and sewing ribbons on both sides so that the cover is adjustable. Attach four ribbons, then tie them up. Your machine will be kept just as neat and clean.

Make me a happy face from felt

Cut out felt shapes for the features and sew or glue them onto the cover.

1

1. Lay the dish towel over the machine, right side facing.

2. Make the back edge level with the bottom of the machine.

3. Fold up the extra cloth at the front so the fold is level with the edge.

This fold will form the pockets.

2

Find the middle by folding the towel in half lengthwise.

Pin the fold in place.

Measure where you want to sew the pockets. Draw chalk lines as guides.

3

Sew along the chalk lines. Reverse stitch at both ends of the lines.

4

Fold the dish towel over so the right sides are facing.

Pin and then baste the side seams in place.

5 Tip for sewing the seams

Place the presser foot against the hemmed edge to help guide your stitching.

6

Finally, remove the basting stitches and turn the cover right side out.

You will need

- Dish towel
- 50in (127cm) ribbon
- Sewing essentials (pages 27–32)

No.5 Shoe bag

Sew a really useful bag.
Simply make a casing for the
ribbon ties and sew the two sides
together—that's all it takes
to make this bag. A silky
ribbon will transform your
bag into something fancy.

A drawstring bag to carry your stuff.

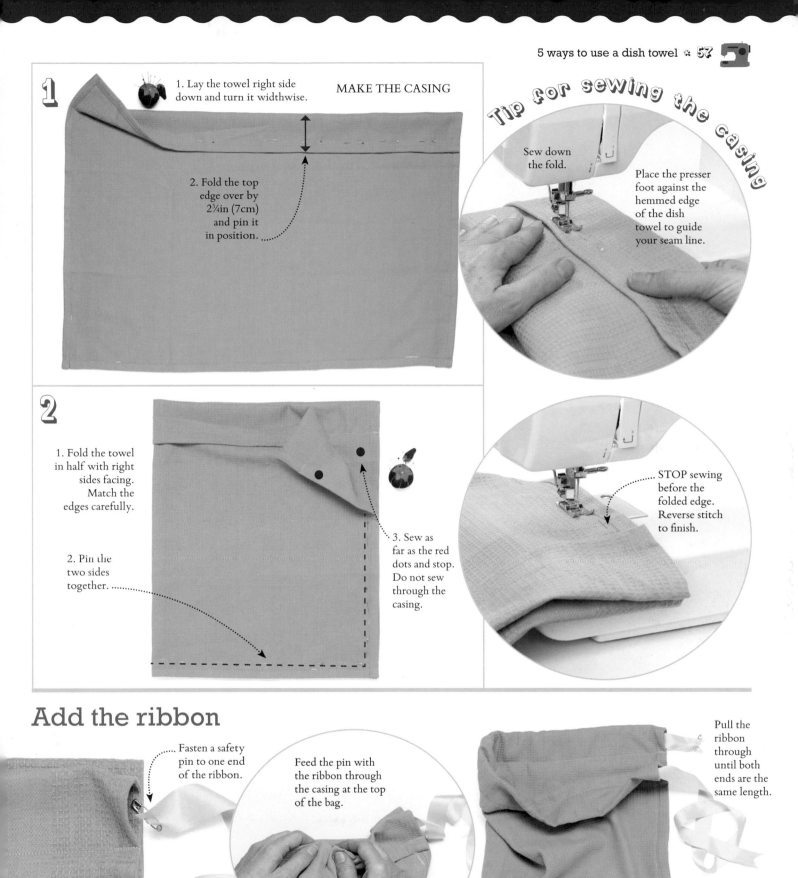

1

1. Lay the towel right side down and turn it widthwise.

MAKE THE CASING

2. Fold the top edge over by 2¾in (7cm) and pin it in position.

Tip for sewing the casing

Sew down the fold.

Place the presser foot against the hemmed edge of the dish towel to guide your seam line.

2

1. Fold the towel in half with right sides facing. Match the edges carefully.

2. Pin the two sides together.

3. Sew as far as the red dots and stop. Do not sew through the casing.

STOP sewing before the folded edge. Reverse stitch to finish.

Add the ribbon

Fasten a safety pin to one end of the ribbon.

Feed the pin with the ribbon through the casing at the top of the bag.

Pull the ribbon through until both ends are the same length.

Finally, remove the pin and turn the bag right side out.

Goodie bags

Simple to make and fun to give. You can save up scraps of pretty fabric and make them into special little gift bags.

You will need

- 2 pieces of 5½ x 7in (15 x 18cm) cotton fabric per bag—change sizes to suit your needs
- Sewing essentials (pages 27–32)

1 Cut out the fabric

Place two pieces of fabric together, wrong sides facing each other.

7in (18cm)

Make a template in the size you want and pin it to the fabric.

5½in (15cm)

Cutting the edges with pinking shears will stop them from fraying.

2 Finishing the bag

Cut two pieces of fabric the same size. Sew along three of the sides, leaving the top open.

To tie up the bag, cut a strip of contrasting fabric long enough to make a bow, or use a ribbon.

No need to turn the corner—just sew straight through the edge of the fabric.

Reverse stitch to secure the ends.

Make it easy pillows

Make a fabric envelope.
This pillow cover doesn't require difficult fastenings. The way the fabric is folded makes an easy opening.

You will need

- 12 x 12in (30 x 30cm) pillow pad
- Cotton fabric
- Trim: rickrack and pom-pom tape
- Sewing essentials (pages 27–32)

What are pillow cushions?

Pillow pads are a handy way to fill your pillow cover. They can be purchased from craft stores and come in different sizes.

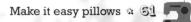

Measuring

Buying a new pillow pad means that you will know exactly what size it is. If you already have a pillow pad, measure it as below to find out what size it is.

Measure across the height and width from seam to seam.

Try it for size

Place the pillow pad onto your piece of fabric and wrap the fabric around the pillow pad to check that you will have enough.

The ends of the fabric should overlap.

1 One piece of fabric

Cut the fabric to the size that fits your pillow pad. For a 12 x 12in (30 x 30cm) pillow pad, cut a piece of fabric 13½ x 30in (35 x 76cm). Place the tracing paper template in the middle of the fabric. Mark the fabric at the edge of the paper.

Handy tip

Cut out a tracing paper template to the size of the pillow pad. This will help to mark where to fold the fabric.

Turn down the fabric edge by 1in (2.5cm) and sew it in place.

TRACING PAPER TEMPLATE

Center the template on the fabric and mark the corners of the paper edges.

Turn up the edge 1in (2.5cm) and sew it in place.

2

Fold the fabric at the marks so that the right sides are facing each other.

3

Pin, then baste, the sides in place.

Stitch both sides with a ½in (12mm) seam allowance.

Turn right side out

Remove the basting stitches and turn the cover right side out.

Firmly work the pad into the cover.

Adjust the pad in the cover to make a good shape.

Clever color combos

Mix it up! To make the most of different pieces of fabric, why not combine three contrasting patterns? Make a feature of how the pillows open with two different fabrics. Add a trim of rickrack or pom-poms for extra flair. Go color crazy!

Somewhere to leave a good read

A pocket to tuck away your music

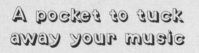

Color combo pillows

This envelope cover is made from three pieces of fabric. The two shorter pieces overlap to make the opening for the pillow pad.

Measure a pillow pad's height and width from seam to seam.

12 x 12in (30 x 30cm)

Fabric measurements allow for the seams and the turnings on the edges.

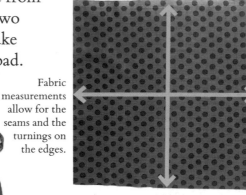

Back: 1 piece of fabric 13 x 13in (33 x 33cm)

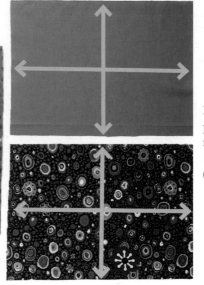

Front: 2 pieces of fabric, each 13 x 9½in (33 x 24cm)

---

1 Place one piece of front fabric wrong side up and turn the top edge down 1in (2.5cm). Pin, then stitch it in place.

Repeat this with the second front piece.

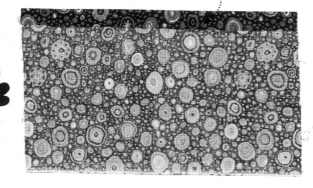

ADDING DECORATION

Pin the trim along the turned edge.

Baste the trim down then machine stitch it in place.

2 Place one piece of front fabric on top of the back piece with right sides facing. Align all the raw (unsewn) edges.

Pin the edges together.

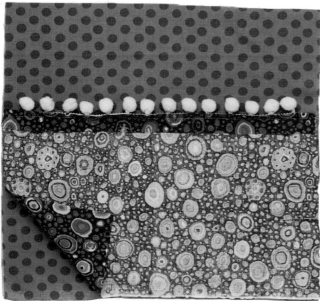

3 Position the second front fabric piece wrong side down, matching the unsewn edges, as shown, and pin it in place.

4 Baste stitch all the layers together around the four outer edges.

Machine stitch all the way around the four edges. Allow ½in (12mm) for the seam allowance.

Turn right side out

Make a whole rainbow of pillow covers

Turn the cover right side out.

Work the pillow pad into the cover.

Adjust the pad inside the pillow so it makes a good shape.

Bobtail rabbits

With their pom-pom tails and creative color combinations, these charming rabbits can show a different side— in a good way. They are made from contrasting fabrics, so flip them around for a whole new look.

Make these simple bunnies in muslin.

Little and large

Change the size of the template to create a family of rabbits. For example, copy the template on this page at 150% or 70% to make a family like one above.

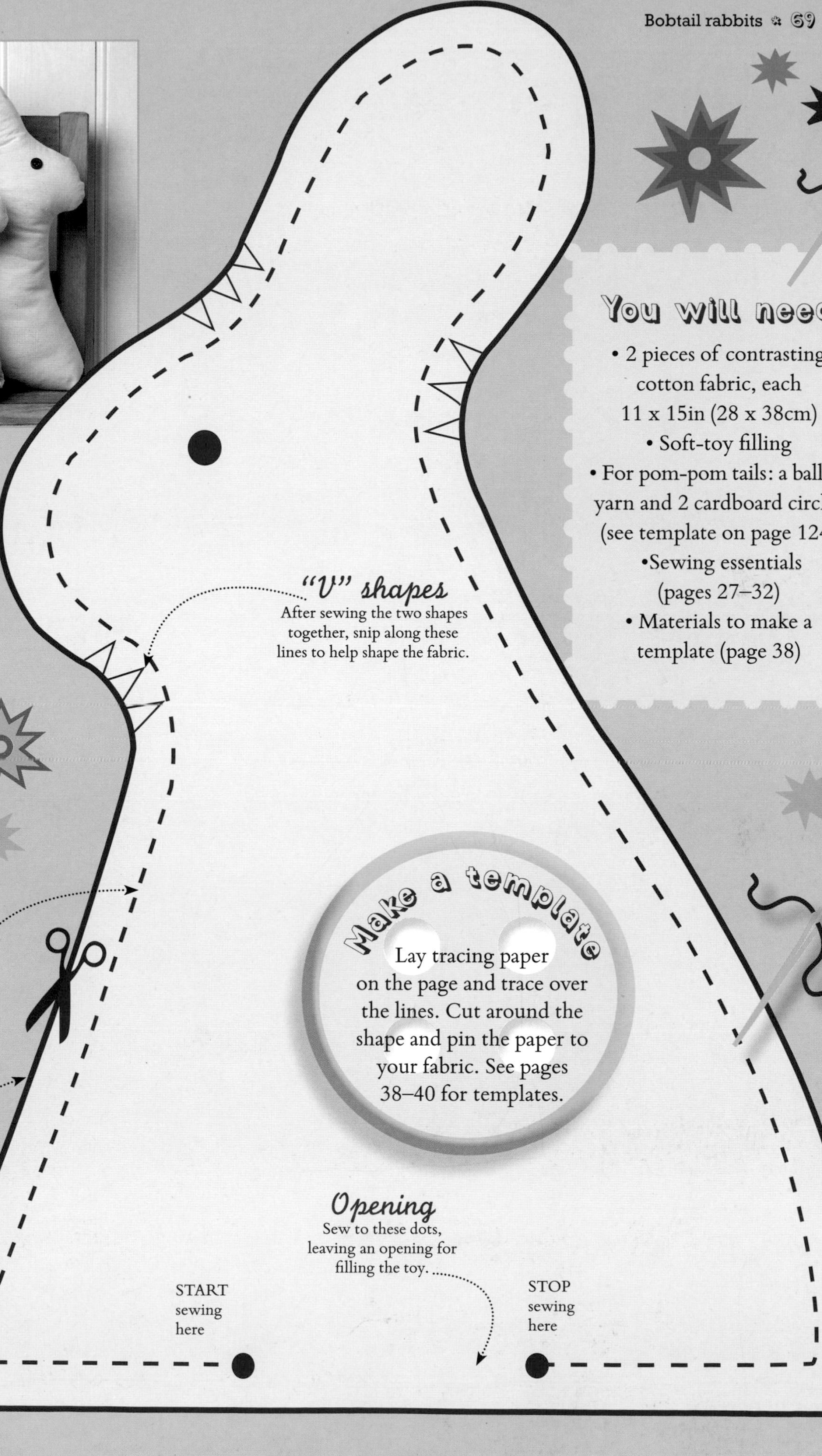

"V" shapes

After sewing the two shapes together, snip along these lines to help shape the fabric.

Make a template

Lay tracing paper on the page and trace over the lines. Cut around the shape and pin the paper to your fabric. See pages 38–40 for templates.

Dotted line

Sew along this line

Solid line

Cut out fabric along this line

Opening

Sew to these dots, leaving an opening for filling the toy...

START sewing here

STOP sewing here

Sew a bobtail

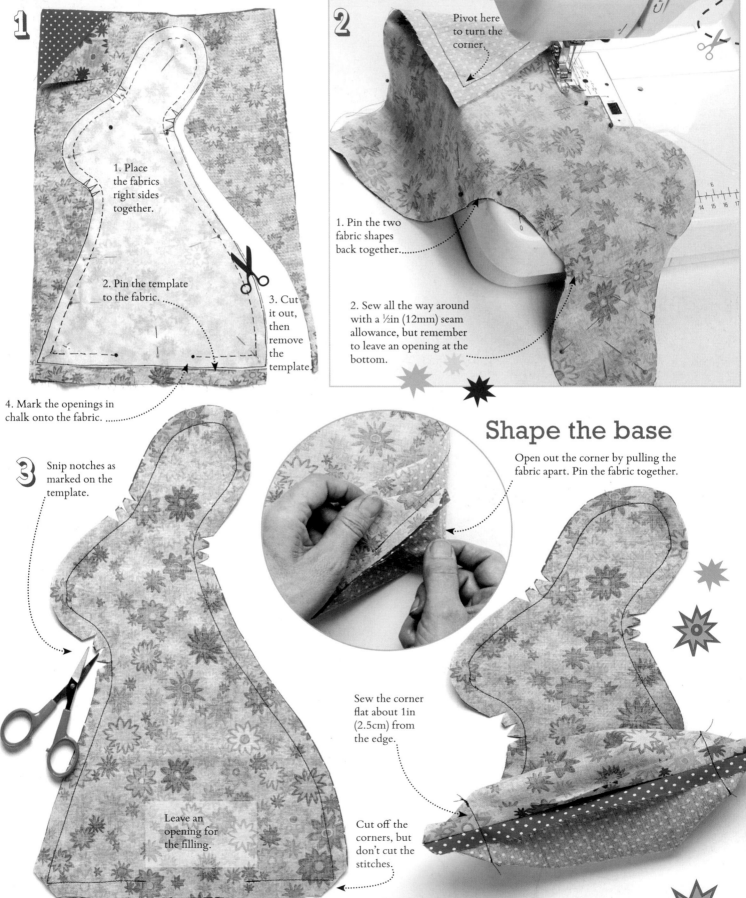

1

1. Place the fabrics right sides together.

2. Pin the template to the fabric.

3. Cut it out, then remove the template.

4. Mark the openings in chalk onto the fabric.

2

Pivot here to turn the corner.

1. Pin the two fabric shapes back together.

2. Sew all the way around with a ½in (12mm) seam allowance, but remember to leave an opening at the bottom.

3 Snip notches as marked on the template.

Leave an opening for the filling.

Shape the base

Open out the corner by pulling the fabric apart. Pin the fabric together.

Sew the corner flat about 1in (2.5cm) from the edge.

Cut off the corners, but don't cut the stitches.

Plump him up

1

Turn the rabbit shape right sides out through the opening. Work a blunt object into all the corners to create a nice shape.

Sewing tip

These rabbits are very curvy and that makes them a little tricky to sew. Remember to take it slow on the machine and carefully move the fabric around the bends.

2

Fill the shape so it feels firm, but not too full.

Fold in the edges of the opening.

3 Carefully pin the fabric together at the opening and neatly sew it with slip stitch.

Now add some finishing touches—buttons for eyes and a pom-pom tail. See the next page to find out how.

Pom-pom tails

1 Make two cardboard circles using the template on page 124. Put the two circles together.

Wrap the yarn around and around the cardboard until all the space is full.

2 Pinch the middle. Slip the scissors between the two circles and cut the yarn.

3 Still holding tight, slide a piece of yarn between the circles. Wrap it around the cut yarn.

4 Pull the yarn tight and knot it securely.

5 Remove the cardboard.

Trim any ragged strands of yarn to neaten up the pom-pom.

6 With a needle and thread, make a few stitches into the pom-pom.

Make a stitch into the fabric of the rabbit where its tail belongs.

To secure the pom-pom, stitch backward and forward through the fabric and the pom-pom. To finish, make two small knots, then cut the thread.

Buttons and bows

Add the finishing touches to your bunny. Measure the rabbit's neck and cut a length of trim slightly longer so that the ends can overlap. Sew the trim in place.

Shapely rabbits

If you haven't shaped the base of your rabbits, or find it too tricky, don't worry. They will still look cute, just not as plump.

Give them contrasting-colored button eyes.

Finish with a ribbon tied in a bow.

Flutterbys

Here are some cheery party streamers. They're made from strips of ribbon stitched to cotton twill tape. They will add a flutter to any occasion.

You will need

- Selection of ribbons, 2yds (2m) of each
- Sewing essentials (pages 27–33)
- 2yds (2m) cotton twill tape

Ready to party!

Ribbon rainbow

Use a rainbow of ribbons like this, or experiment a little. Try leftover scraps in all kinds of shades and textures. Once the ribbons are all fluttering, they'll look pretty.

How to make Flutterbys

1

Cut out strips of ribbon about 8in (20cm) long

The ribbons don't have to be the same length. Vary lengths for the different colors.

Trim one end, as shown here.

2

Trimming the ribbons adds a nice touch, and it stops them from fraying.

3

1. Make a loop in the end of the tape by folding it over 8in (20cm) and pinning it in place.

2. Pin the top of each ribbon to the middle of the tape about a ribbon-width apart.

3. Continue adding ribbons. Make a loop at the other end of the tape in the same way.

4

First, sew down the end of the tape to make the loop.

Then, sew the ribbons in place, gently feeding the tape through and removing the pins as you go.

TIP

Take it slow—there's no need for speed.

5

Fold the tape in half to cover the ribbon tops and pin it in place.

6

Sew the tape down to sandwich the ribbons in between. Remove the pins as you go.

How to make Bunting

find the template for Bunting on page 124

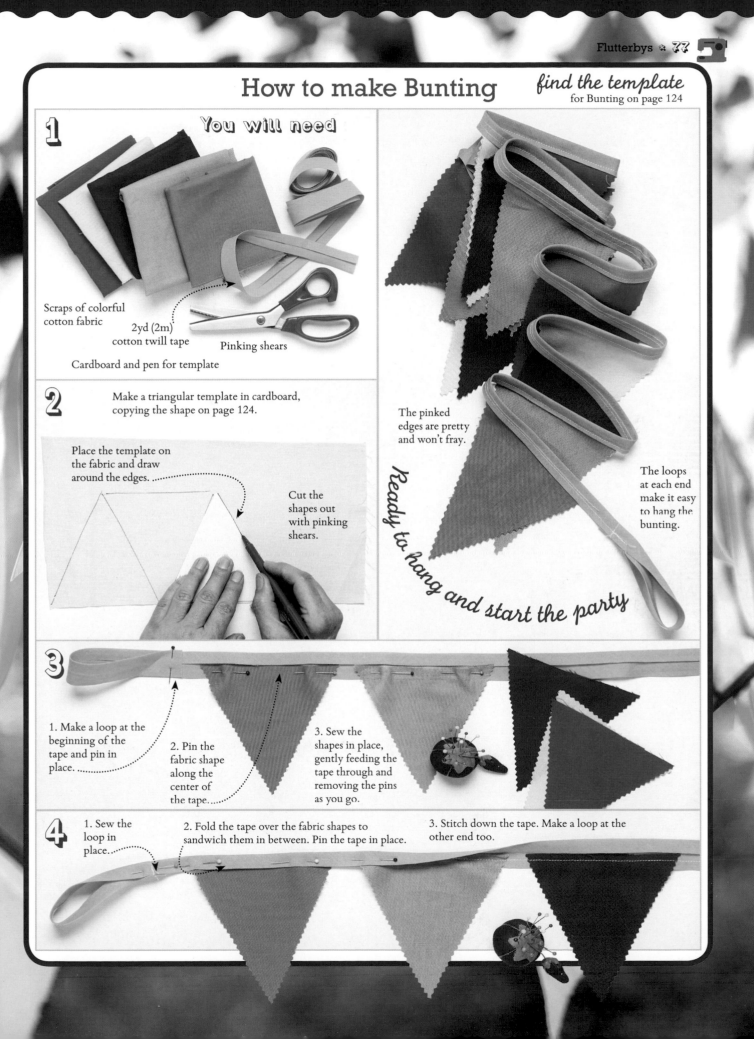

1 You will need

Scraps of colorful cotton fabric

2yd (2m) cotton twill tape

Pinking shears

Cardboard and pen for template

The pinked edges are pretty and won't fray.

The loops at each end make it easy to hang the bunting.

Ready to hang and start the party

2

Make a triangular template in cardboard, copying the shape on page 124.

Place the template on the fabric and draw around the edges.

Cut the shapes out with pinking shears.

3

1. Make a loop at the beginning of the tape and pin in place.

2. Pin the fabric shape along the center of the tape.

3. Sew the shapes in place, gently feeding the tape through and removing the pins as you go.

4

1. Sew the loop in place.

2. Fold the tape over the fabric shapes to sandwich them in between. Pin the tape in place.

3. Stitch down the tape. Make a loop at the other end too.

Handy bags

These simple cotton bags will hold all your odds and ends. Make them as big or as small as you need— the instructions for making them is the same no matter the size.

You will need
MEDIUM BAG:

- 16 x 10½in
(40 x 27cm) cotton fabric
- Ribbon 25in (64cm) long
- Sewing essentials (pages 27–32)

Bags of sizes

LARGE BAG:
- 20 x 12½in (50 x 31cm)
cotton fabric • Ribbon 32in
(80cm) long

SMALL BAG:
- 14 x 7½in (35 x 19cm) cotton
fabric • Ribbon 23in
(58cm) long

Cut out the fabric

Large bag

Medium bag

Small bag

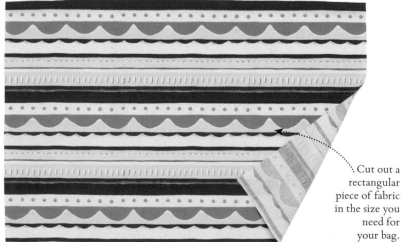

Cut out a rectangular piece of fabric in the size you need for your bag.

1 Sew the bag

1. Turn the top edge over ⅜in (10mm) and press it flat.

Fold the fabric in half with right sides together and pin, matching the edges.

STOP stitching here.

START stitching here.

Use a ½in (12mm) seam allowance.

2 Make a casing

Fold the top edge over ¾in (2cm) and pin in place.

Cut off the corners, but don't cut the stitches.

Sew along the two marked sides, pivoting the needle at the corner.

Stop stitching here. Reverse stitch to finish.

Press the seam flat.

Sew the folded edge down.

NOTE: To allow room for the bag to fit under the needle, remove the extension table from your sewing machine.

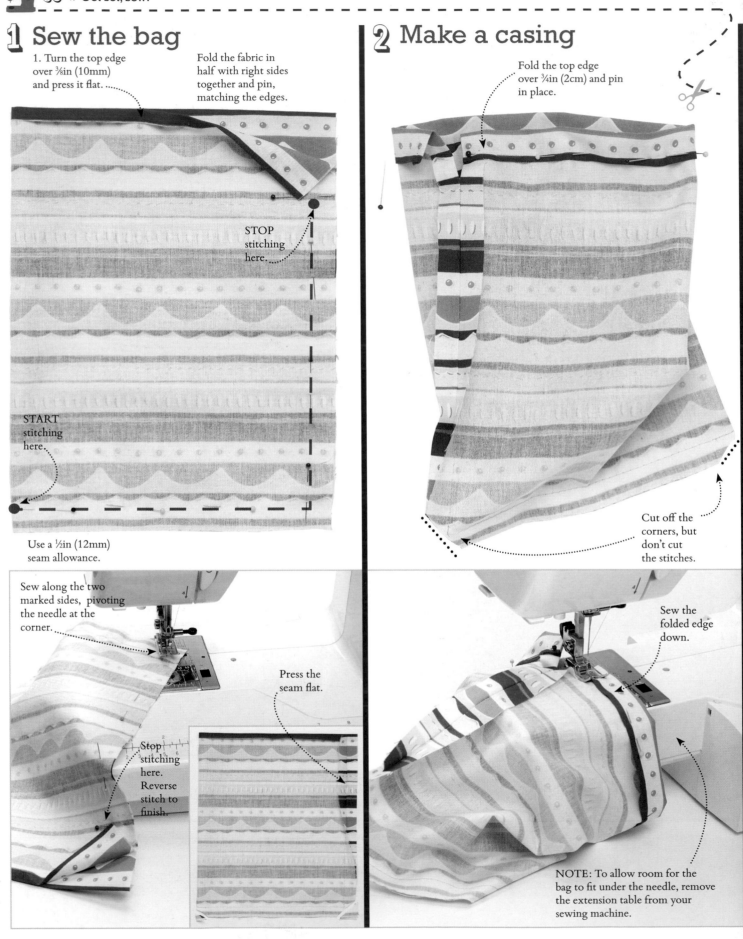

3 Turn right side out

Turn the bag
right side out.

Fasten a safety pin to
one end of the
ribbon.

The ribbon
goes all the
way through
the casing.

4 Insert the ribbon

Place the pin at the
opening of the
casing.

Work the pin through
the casing.

Bring the pin and the ribbon all
the way around and out the
other side.

Even up the
two ends of
the ribbon and
remove the pin.

Big Peg
That's me!

Who is Big Peg?

She's a big pillow. Her body is made from a rectangular pillow pad instead of toy filling. Her clothes are made the same way as Square Peg's. She's big and luvable.

Square Peg and friends

Have some fun with this rag doll and her pals. She's like a pillow with arms and legs. Her top, skirt, and even her legs and shoes are made all-in-one— so she comes dressed and ready.

We're getting carried away :)

Square Peg
That's me!

Square Peg's templates

To make the templates lay tracing paper over the page and trace out all of the lines. Cut out the paper shapes and pin them to your fabrics. Use the same template piece for the skirt and top, just use different fabrics for each.

Solid line
Cut fabric out along these lines

Head

CUT 2

Dotted line
Sew along these lines

FOLD Line

Join this edge to the ARMS

Hands

CUT 2

TOP: Join this edge to the HEAD

SKIRT: Join this edge to the TOP

Top

CUT 2

Skirt

CUT 2

TIP: Use this same pattern piece for both the TOP and the SKIRT, cut two of each.

FOLD Line

Arms

CUT 2

Join this edge to the HAND

TOP: Join this edge to the SKIRT

Come and meet my friends.

Fold lines

Fold your fabric, then pin the paper template to the fabric, placing the fold line on the fold of the fabric. Don't cut through the fold!

FOLD Line

Legs

CUT 2

Join this edge to the FOOT

Join this edge to the LEG

FOLD Line

Feet

CUT 2

Different sizes

All Square Peg's friends are made with the same templates and instructions. If you like the idea of a larger doll, just enlarge the templates on a copier to any size you want.

You will need

- Cotton fabric:
  HEAD: 8 x 10in (20 x 26cm)
  TOP and SKIRT: 8 x 10in
  (20 x 26cm) each
  LEGS: 10 x 8in (26 x 20cm)
  FEET: 8 x 5in (20 x 13cm)
  ARMS: 10 x 5in (26 x 13cm)
  HANDS: 3 x 10in (7 x 26cm)
- Soft-toy filling
- Ribbons and trim
- Permanent marker for face
- Sewing essentials (pages 27–32)

Prepare the doll's body parts

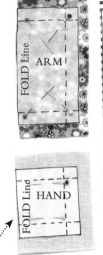

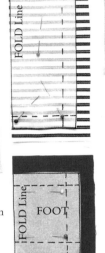

Remember to fold the fabric in half for the leg, foot, arm, and hand shapes.

1

Pin the paper pieces to the fabric and cut them out. Don't cut through the folds.

Cut out each shape

2

Cut out two sets of each shape.

Square Peg likes to chat with her sister.

Join the fabric

1

Place the fabrics right sides together. ....

Open up all the folded pieces.

Pin the foot to the leg.

Pin the hand to the arm.

Pin the head and top together, then the skirt to the other side of the top.

2

Baste, then sew all the pieces of fabric together. Allow ½in (12mm) for the seam allowance.

3

Make two sets of leg, arm, and body pieces.

Press all the seams open.

Make two legs and arms

1

Fold the fabric over lengthwise and pin in position. ....

Baste stitch along the long edge and the end of the foot and hand. Do not sew the tops of the arms or legs.

2

Sew along the basted edges, allowing ¼in (7mm) for the seam allowance. ...

Turn the arms and legs right side out. Shape the corners with a blunt tool.

3

Fill all the limb parts with toy filling, leaving the ends open.

Don't overfill them. Keep the arms and legs soft and bendy.

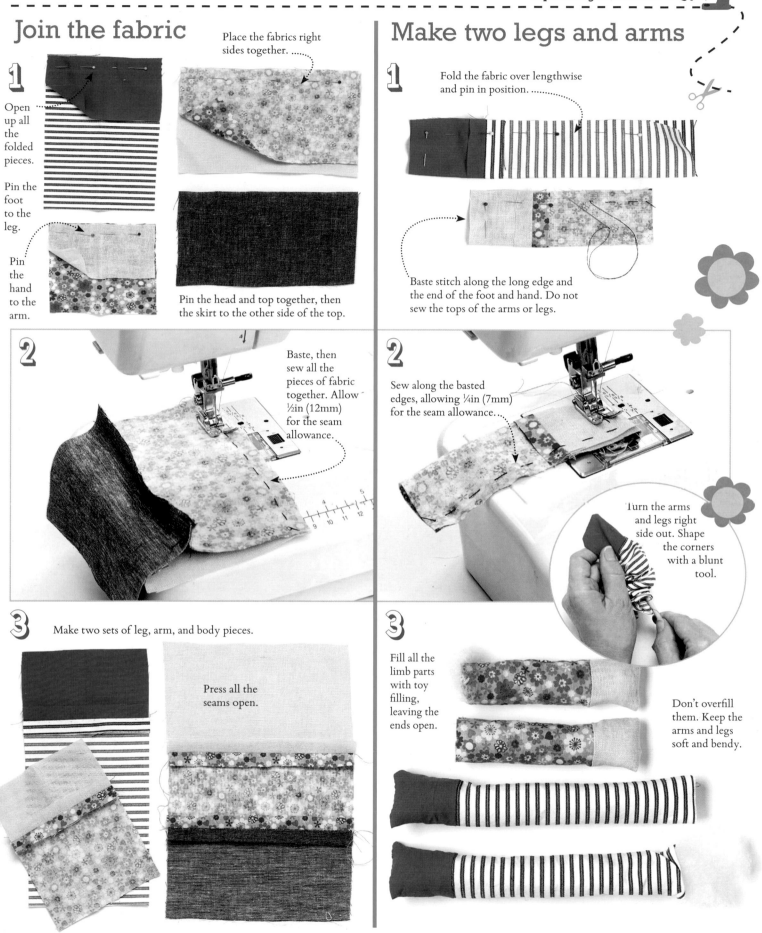

Make Peg's body

1

Lay the body fabric right side up with the head at the top....

Align the top edge of the legs to the bottom edge of the fabric and pin them in place, as shown.

Baste them securely in position.

2

Make sure to place the fabric with right sides facing each other.

Lay the other body piece over the legs

Pin, then baste, the fabric together at the bottom.

3

Sew all the layers of fabric together.

Carefully feed the fabric through the machine to keep the legs in place as you sew.

4

Open up the fabric and lay it flat. Position the open ends of the arms either side of the body, as shown.

Handy tip

Fold over the top edge of the head fabric and press it flat. This helps later when finishing the doll.

Pin, then baste, them in place ready for sewing.

5

Place the body fabrics together again.

Pin the sides then baste the edges together, making sure the arms are positioned inside. Leave the top of the head open.

6

Sew all the layers of fabric together on both sides.

Carefully feed the fabric through the machine to keep the legs and arms in place as you sew. You don't want them to get caught in the stitches.

Turning out

Turn the doll's body right side out. Work out the corners of the skirt to make a good shape.

Add the filling

Add the soft-toy filling evenly, don't overfill. Leave room to sew up the top.

Pin the top edges together and sew the opening closed with slip stitch.

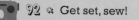

Making faces and decorating

To make a face, draw the eyes and mouth directly on the fabric with a permanent felt-tip marker. Draw the features in chalk or pencil first if you like. Finish your doll by sewing ribbons and trim in place.

How to make Big Peg

The only difference between this doll and her small friends is her size. The way you make her is the same. Once you've enlarged the template, cut the fabric and follow the same steps for Square Peg.

Pillow body

This doll's body is made using a 12 x 16in (30 x 40cm) pillow pad.

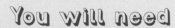

You will need

- Enough cotton fabric for the head, top, skirt, legs, and arms
- Pillow pad
- Soft-toy filling for legs and arms
- Ribbon and trim for decoration
- Felt-tip markers to make a face
- Sewing essentials (pages 27–32)

Finishing Big Peg

Enlarge the template by 200% on a photo copier. Print out the template. Cut out the paper pieces and pin them directly to the fabric. Prepare the fabric pieces and assemble them by following the same steps for Square Peg. Once the arms and legs are turned out, fill the body with the pillow pad and close the opening with slip stitch. Finally, add bows and trim and draw on her face.

Pin watch

No more losing pins! Now you'll have them handy when you're busy at the sewing machine. This "watch" is a safe place to keep pins and the cardboard insert will stop them from poking you... Ouch!!!

Velcro
Stitch Velcro® to each end of the ribbon so that you can fasten it around your wrist.

You will need

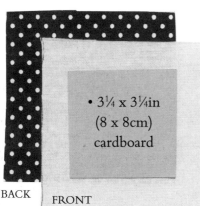

BACK   FRONT

• 3¼ x 3¼in (8 x 8cm) cardboard

• 2 pieces of 4 x 4in (10 x 10cm) cotton fabric
• Cotton twill tape or ribbon 1in (2.5cm) wide for wristband • Loop and hook tape (Velcro®)
• Soft-toy filling • Sewing essentials (pages 27–32)
• Black felt-tip pen for watch face

Sewing tip
Because the pincushion is small, sewing on the machine can be tricky. Take your time and position the work carefully before stitching.

Watch face
Using a felt-tip pen, simply draw a watch face onto the fabric. Or, you can draw any picture you want.

Ribbon
Thick cotton tape works well for the wristband. Cut it with pinking shears.

find the template for Pin watch on page 124

How to make a pincushion

Measure your wrist and cut the ribbon long enough to allow for the ends to overlap for the fastening.

········· Pin the ribbon to the center of the fabric.

Stitch a rectangle shape to secure the ribbon.

1 Sewing backward and forward at each corner will help secure the ribbon. ····

2 Fold the ends of the ribbon in so they're clear of the pins. ······

Pin the fabric right sides together.

3 Pivot the needle at the corners. ····

Allow ¼in (7mm) for the seam allowance.

Sew around three sides only.

4 Snip off the corners and turn the fabric right sides out.

The ribbon will now be on the outside. ·········

5 Insert the piece of cardboard.

6 Add filling between the cardboard and the front.

7 Fold the edge of the fabric over and pin the opening ··· closed.

Use slip stitch to close up the opening. Draw a watch face or another design of your choice.

Pins always on hand

Fasten the band around your wrist and start sewing.

Garlands

Drape these colorful garlands around your room. String them across a window or use them to brighten up any space.

You will need

- Scraps of colorful felt

- Templates cut from cardboard
  LARGE: 2in (5cm)
  SMALL: 1in (2.5cm)

- Sewing essentials (pages 27–32)

1 Place the templates on the felt and carefully trace around the edge.

Felt-tip pen

Cut out the felt circles. You can use pinking shears to give a decorative edge. Cut as many felt circles as you like.

2 Pull out long thread ends. Position the circles under the foot and sew down the center.

Have the next circle ready to sew. Do not cut the thread in between. Carefully feed the circles through and flatten down the felt as you sew.

When you run out of circles, pull out the thread ends and cut the garland free from the machine. Use the threads to hang the garlands.

Mix up the sizes and colors. Stack a small and large circle together and sew small circles on each side, or whatever sequence you want.

Templates

Trace around the circles below to make your templates.

LARGE

SMALL

Floppy pots

Keep things neat. There's no need for clutter when you can create these fun storage pots. Just two pieces of fabric (a pretty cotton backed with muslin) is all it takes to keep these containers sturdy and upright. Once you've made one pot you won't be able to stop.

You will need

- 1 piece of cotton fabric
  12 x 7in (31 x 18cm)
- 1 piece of muslin or thick cotton fabric
  12 x 7in (31 x 18cm)
- Sewing essentials (pages 27–32)

Muslin

Cotton fabric

Make a pot to store all your sewing odds and ends.

Pot sizes

To make bigger pots, simply cut out larger rectangular shapes of fabric. This pot is 16 x 10in (42 x 25cm).

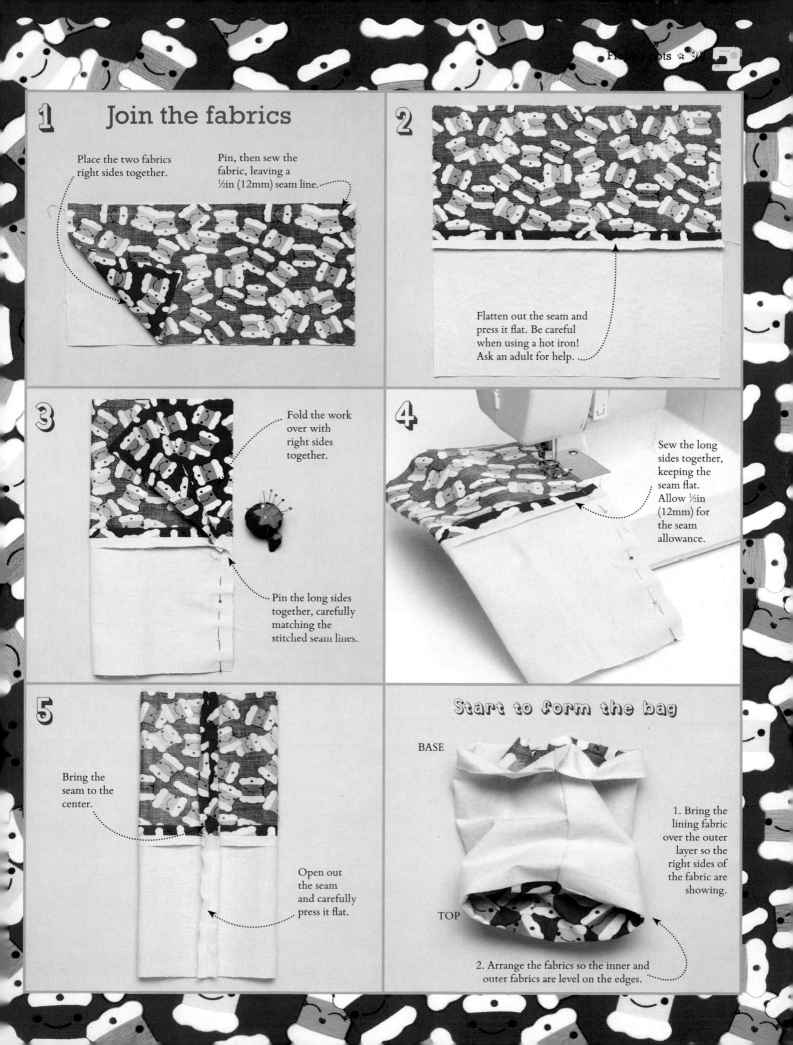

1 Join the fabrics

Place the two fabrics right sides together.

Pin, then sew the fabric, leaving a ½in (12mm) seam line.

2

Flatten out the seam and press it flat. Be careful when using a hot iron! Ask an adult for help.

3

Fold the work over with right sides together.

Pin the long sides together, carefully matching the stitched seam lines.

4

Sew the long sides together, keeping the seam flat. Allow ½in (12mm) for the seam allowance.

5

Bring the seam to the center.

Open out the seam and carefully press it flat.

Start to form the bag

BASE

TOP

1. Bring the lining fabric over the outer layer so the right sides of the fabric are showing.

2. Arrange the fabrics so the inner and outer fabrics are level on the edges.

1 Finish the top edge

Neaten the top edge of the pot so that the seam runs along the top.

Pin it in place.

2

Remove the extension table on the machine.

Slide the bag over the machine and topstitch around the pinned edge.

1 Make the base

Position the side seam at the center back.

Pin, then stitch the base of the bag together.

2

To create the bottom of the bag, pinch in the corners, as shown.

Pin the corners in place.

3

Sew across both corners.

Turn right side out

Work into the corners to make the base a good shape.

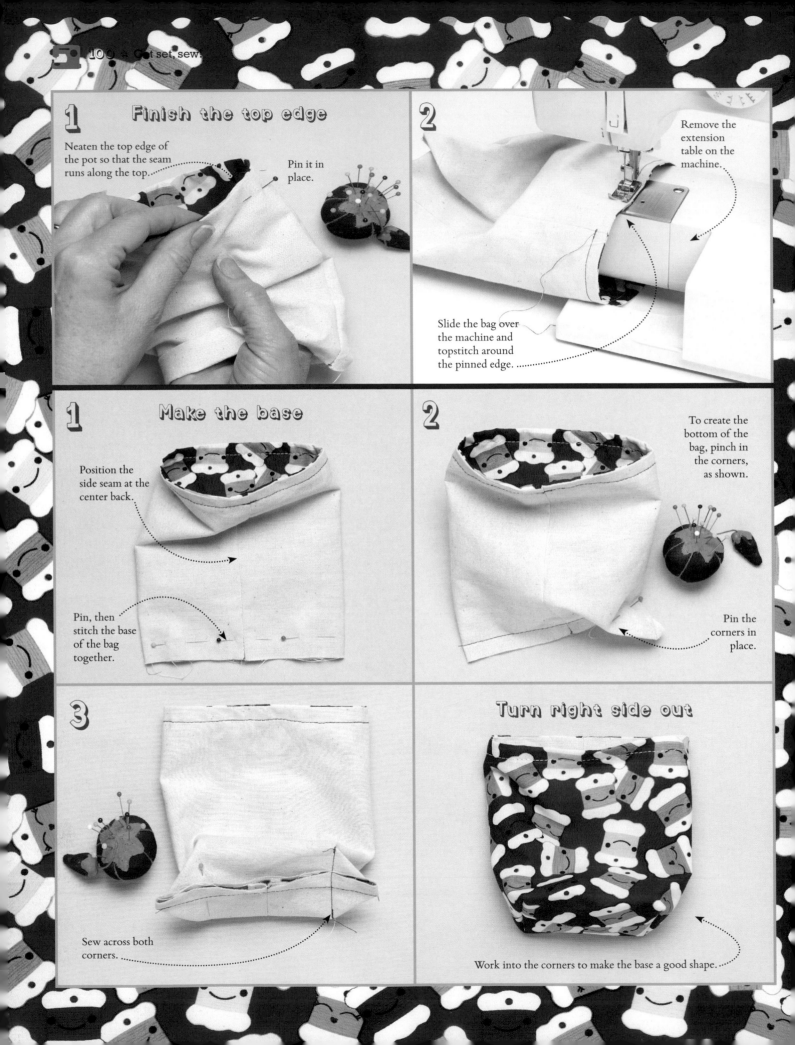

* Keep the place neat * Start filling your pots *

Turning down the top helps make the pots sturdy.

Playful pups

These cuddly pooches make cute little toys, or you can enlarge them to make comfy pillows.

Pup's family
To make a pillow-sized pup, photocopy the template and increase it to 150%, or larger if you want.

Dotted line
Sew along this line.

Make a template

Lay tracing paper on the page and trace over the lines. Cut around the shape and pin the paper to the fabric. Pages 38–40 have template information.

START sewing here.

Opening
Sew to these dots, leaving an opening to fill the toy.

STOP sewing here.

Solid line
Cut the fabric out along this line.

"V" shapes
After sewing the two shapes together, snip along these lines to help shape the fabric.

1

1. Place two pieces of fabric with right sides facing.

2. Make a paper template and pin it to the fabrics.

3. Mark the dots on the fabric.

4. Cut out the fabric shapes.

2

Mark with chalk where to leave the opening.

Sew the shapes together.

You will need

• Template

• 2 pieces of cotton fabric, each 13 x 9in (33 x 23cm) for Pup's body • Felt for the ears and collar
• 3 buttons for the eyes and nose • Soft-toy filling
• Sewing essentials (pages 27–32)

3 Snip the notches into the fabric and cut off the corners. Don't cut through the stitches.

Leave the opening for filling.

4 Turn the shape right side out.

Use a knitting needle or other blunt object to work into all the corners, especially the tail.

5 1. Stuff the shape starting with the tail, head, and legs.

3. Close the opening using slip stitch.

2. Use the needle to work the stuffing into the corners.

Add ears and eyes

Sew on button eyes and nose.

Draw a mouth with a marker.

Cut out two felt ears and sew them to the head.

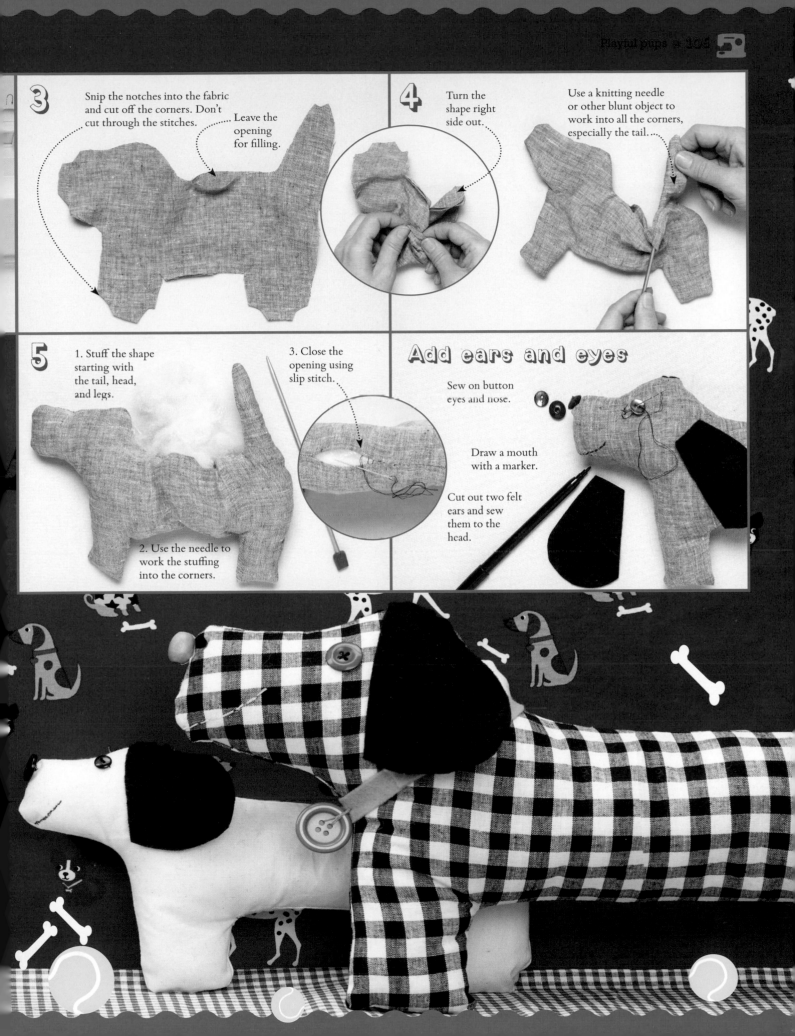

Wacky ornaments

Take your machine for a walk! Just twist and turn the fabric under the needle while changing stitches and thread colors. It's a fun way to decorate any other project, too.

1 Move the felt around and around to make a random stitch pattern.

Change stitch styles too.

2 Make a 5in (12cm) cardboard circle.

Place the cardboard over the area you want to cut and draw around the circle.

3 Cut out the felt circle.

4 Cut out another circle of felt for the back.

Pin the two circles together.

5 Stuff the ornament.

Sew the two circles together, leaving a gap in the stitches for the soft-toy filling.

6 Hand sew the opening closed. Attach a ribbon loop and a button.

Finish the edge with pinking shears.

Sewing tip
When changing stitch styles, ALWAYS remember to lift the needle out of fabric first, or the needle could break.

Zip it!

Quiet now! Keep these little purses zipped so all your treasures stay safe. Create crazy characters using zippers for mouths.

Hey!
What did you say?

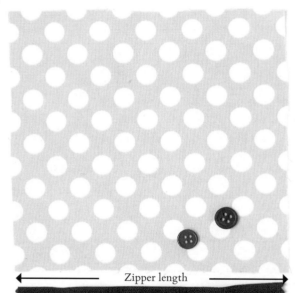

Zipper length

You will need

• Zipper at least 4in (10cm)

• 2 pieces cotton fabric cut to the same width of the zipper and a height of your choice

• 2 buttons for eyes
• A piece of ribbon (optional)

• Sewing essentials (pages 27–32)

Tips on zippers

Zippers are a clever way of fastening two pieces of fabric together. They are readily available in craft stores. For this project, choose metal or plastic teeth. Zippers for skirts are about the right length—5–6in (10–15cm). There is no need to change the foot on your machine to a zipper foot—just sew carefully with the normal foot.

Look at me, I'm a circle with ears.

What a mouthful

Wide or narrow—the width of these bags is based on the length of the zipper you have. Change the depth of your bag with different sizes of fabric. Try two different fabrics to set the top head piece apart from the lower body piece.

1 Sew in the zipper

Lay out the fabrics right sides up with the edges touching, but not overlapping.

Place the zipper where the two fabrics touch.

Pin, then baste the edges of the zipper to the fabric. Baste one edge to the top fabric and the other edge to the bottom fabric.

2

Position the zipper under the needle ready to stitch near the edge of the zipper fabric.

Edge of fabric

Pull

TIP: Sewing near the edge of the zipper fabric will allow the sewing foot to move past the zipper pull with ease.

3

Pin, then baste the other end of the fabric pieces right sides together.

Open the zipper halfway.

Z Z z z zip

I've got a small head.

Big or small head?

This depends on where you put the zipper before joining the side seams in step 5. If you want a small head, lay out the work so the zipper is above the center line.

To make a round head, stitch the side seams into curves instead of straight edges.

4 Stitch the basted edges of the fabrics together.

The pieces of fabric are now joined at both ends. Open out the seam and press it flat.

5 Move the zipper around so it's just above the center of the work. Lay the work flat, as below. ....

Pin, then stitch the two side edges using a ½in (12mm) seam allowance.

6 Carefully trim the corners, then turn the work right side out through the zipper. Do not cut the stitches.

7 Add buttons for the eyes and a nose. Be sure to sew the buttons to the top layer of fabric only.

Sew buttons in place with a needle and thread.

Attach a ribbon to the zipper pull.

My head is not big.

Ribbons help you open the zipper easily. ....

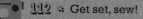
3-D chickens

It's like magic! You can transform two squares of fabric into these shapely chickens. Try mixing up your fabrics to make a colorful brood.

Find the template
for the chickens on page 124.

You will need

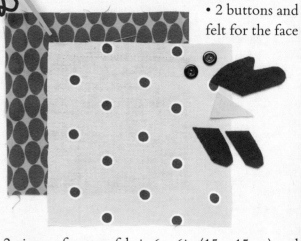

- 2 buttons and felt for the face
- 2 pieces of cotton fabric 6 x 6in (15 x 15cm) each
- Sewing essentials (pages 27–32) • Soft-toy filling

Chicken size

To make larger or smaller chickens, just cut out different-sized squares and follow the steps below.

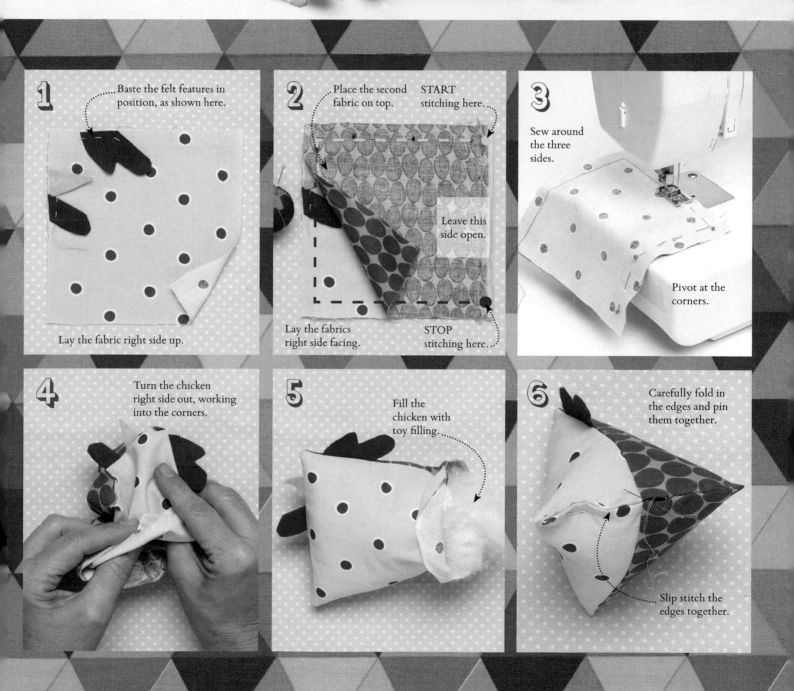

1 Baste the felt features in position, as shown here.

Lay the fabric right side up.

2 ..Place the second fabric on top.

START stitching here..

Leave this side open.

Lay the fabrics right side facing.

STOP stitching here..

3 Sew around the three sides.

Pivot at the corners.

4 Turn the chicken right side out, working into the corners.

5 Fill the chicken with toy filling..

6 Carefully fold in the edges and pin them together.

Slip stitch the edges together.

Good night, Ted, close your eyes and go to sleep. ZZZ

Sleep well, Ted

Make a comfy bed for your dolls or Ted. Find a box that's just the right size and create a bedspread and an array of matching pillows.

How to make Ted's bedspread

This cover is made from three squares of cotton fabric. Choose two colorful cottons—one each for the front and back—and a plain white fabric for the lining. The lining will help make the cover fuller and will stop the patterned fabric from showing through to the other side.

You will need

- For the bedspread: 3 pieces of cotton fabric 13½ x 13½in (35 x 35cm) each for the front, lining, and back
- Selection of ribbons and trim 13½in (35cm) long
- Sewing essentials (pages 27–32)

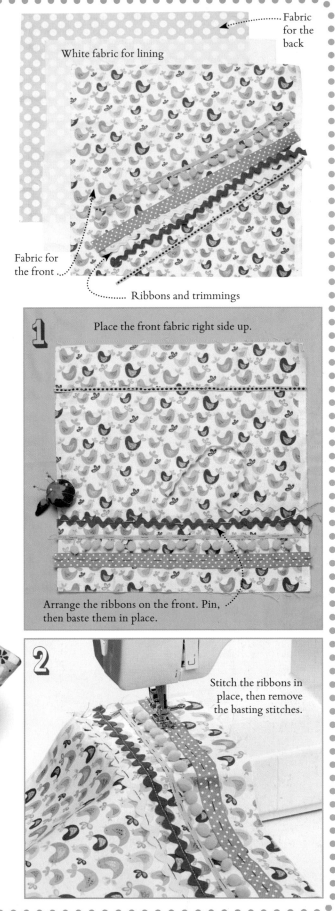

Fabric for the back

White fabric for lining

Fabric for the front

Ribbons and trimmings

1 Place the front fabric right side up.

Arrange the ribbons on the front. Pin, then baste them in place.

2 Stitch the ribbons in place, then remove the basting stitches.

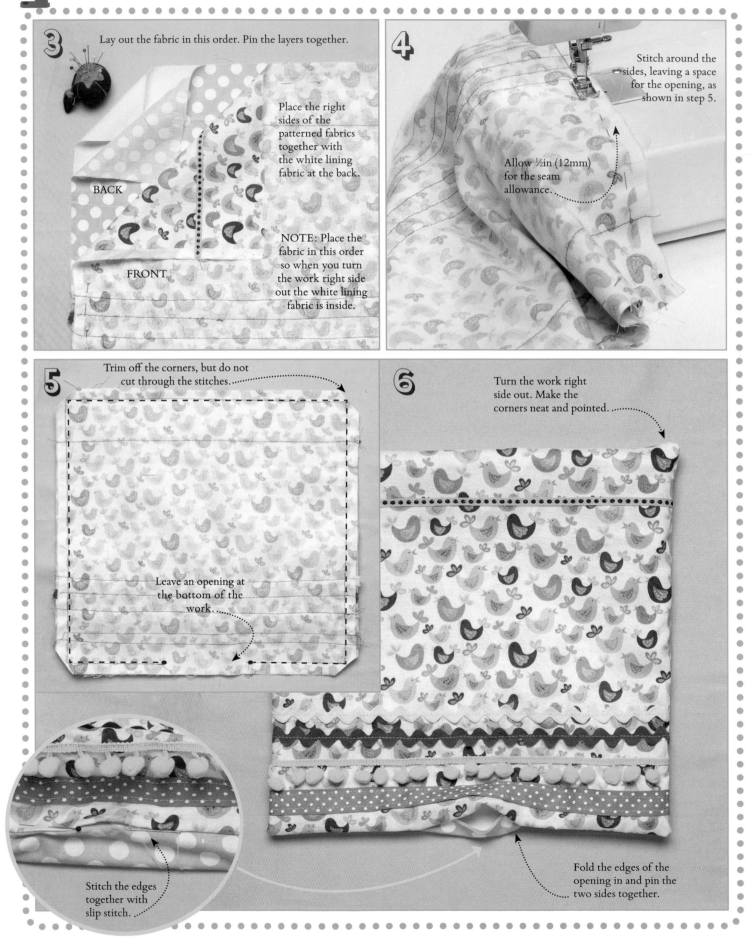

3 Lay out the fabric in this order. Pin the layers together.

Place the right sides of the patterned fabrics together with the white lining fabric at the back.

BACK

FRONT

NOTE: Place the fabric in this order so when you turn the work right side out the white lining fabric is inside.

4 Stitch around the sides, leaving a space for the opening, as shown in step 5.

Allow ½in (12mm) for the seam allowance.

5 Trim off the corners, but do not cut through the stitches.

Leave an opening at the bottom of the work.

6 Turn the work right side out. Make the corners neat and pointed.

Fold the edges of the opening in and pin the two sides together.

Stitch the edges together with slip stitch.

How to make Ted's pillows

The pillows can be made big or small by cutting different sized fabric. The fabric at the back overlaps, so no need for any fastening. The round pillow is a fun addition, finished off with a button in the middle on both sides.

You will need

- Large pillow:
18 x 6in (46 x 15cm) cotton fabric
- Round pillow:
Two 4¾in (12cm) circles of cotton fabric
- Soft-toy filling
- Sewing essentials (pages 27–32)

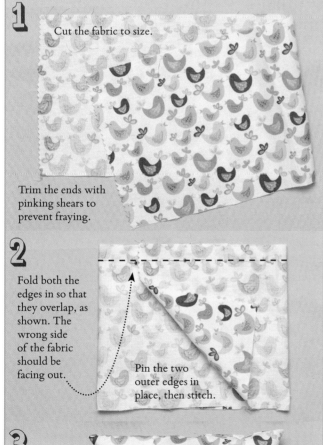

1 Cut the fabric to size.

Trim the ends with pinking shears to prevent fraying.

2 Fold both the edges in so that they overlap, as shown. The wrong side of the fabric should be facing out.

Pin the two outer edges in place, then stitch.

3 Turn the pillow right side out through the opening. Fill the pillow until it's soft and squishy.

1 Cut out two circles.

2 Pin the circles right sides together.

3 1. Sew together, leaving space for an opening.

2. Cut V notches around the edges.

4 Turn the pillow right side out and fill.

5
1. Close the opening with slip stitch.

2. Attach the buttons by working the needle from the front to the back through the buttons.

Monster invasion

They arrived from a land that time forgot, with their staring eyes and bright patterns! Really though, they're just old softies. And who can resist a bunch of colorful ribbon tags?

You will need

- Sewing essentials (pages 27–32)
- Monster template
- Wobbly eyes or buttons
- Strips of ribbon
- Soft-toy filling
- Cotton fabric to fit the size of the template

1

1. Fold the ribbons in half.

2. Position them around the top edge of the fabric. The cut ends should sit on the edge of the fabric.

3. Pin in place.

NOTE: Place the fabric with the right side facing you.

2

1. Baste the ribbons down.

2. Lay the other piece of fabric over the top, right sides together.

3. Pin together, then machine sew, leaving the bottom open.

3

Remove the basting thread, then turn the right way out.

Sewing tip

Remember in Step 1 to place the ribbons on the right side of the fabric, with the folded edge facing the center. That way, they will be turned the right way out once you've sewn them.

4

1. Stuff with the soft-toy filling.

2. Turn in the raw edges and close the opening using slip stitch.

3. Sew or glue on the eyes. Add as many as you like to make your monster look more alienlike.

1

Fold the fabric with the right sides facing. Pin the template in position, then cut around it.

2

3. Fold the ribbons in half and pin to the fabric, as shown here.

Cut the ribbons 5½in (14cm) long.

2. Mark out the ribbon positions with chalk.

1. Unpin the two pieces. Lay one of the fabric pieces right side up.

3

1. Baste the ribbons down.

2. Position the other fabric piece over the top with right sides facing each other and pin in place.

3. Mark with chalk where to leave the opening.

TIP:

By placing the ribbons on the right side of the fabric with the folded part facing inward, the folded ribbons will stand up along the seam when the final piece is turned out.

4

Sew all the way around, leaving a space for filling.

Go slowly around the shape and pivot the fabric to get a good point on the tail. Don't catch the folded ends of the ribbons in the stitches.

5

Turn the shape right side out.

Work into the corners to make a good shape.

Use a knitting needle to push the tail out.

Add the filling, working it into the tail and head first.

Making monster friends

All the monsters are made the same way—only the shapes are different. Choose one of them, then copy a template from page 122. Cut fabric to size and follow the instructions.

Make a face

Stitch the eyes in place.

Cut out a felt mouth and sew that on as well.

Repeat the face on the other side of his head so he can look both ways.

Monster shapes

Shapely creatures can be difficult to make. Sew slowly on the machine, edge your way around the bends, and pivot the fabric at the corners. Don't worry if your monster turns out a bit lopsided. Remember, he's from another planet, so is bound to look strange.

Monster shapes

Lay tracing paper over the monster you want to make. Trace over all the lines. Cut out the paper shape and pin it to your fabric.

The Blob

Template is actual size

Big Monster

To make Big Monster the same size as the one shown in the main photograph, you will need to increase this template on a photocopier by 130%.

All the monster instructions can be found on pages 118–121.

Plodosaurus

To make Plodosaurus the same size as
the one shown in the main photograph,
you will need to increase this template
on a photocopier by 130%.

Wobbles

Template is actual size

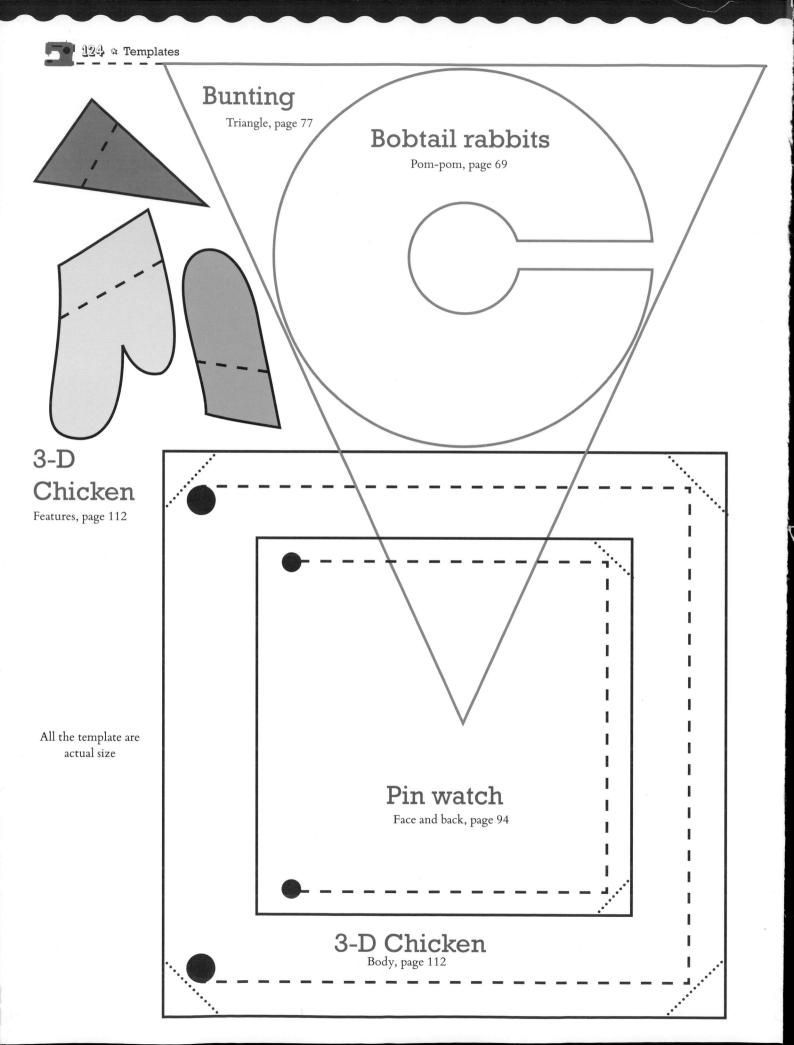

Bunting

Triangle, page 77

Bobtail rabbits

Pom-pom, page 69

3-D Chicken

Features, page 112

All the template are
actual size

Pin watch

Face and back, page 94

3-D Chicken

Body, page 112

Index

3-D chickens 112-113

• A •
apron 52-53

• B •
bags
goodie bags 58-59
handy bags 78-81
shoe bag 56-57
tote bag 48-49
zip it! 108-111
basting stitch 36
removing 37
bobbin 16-17, 29
filling 16
loading 17
bobtail rabbits 68-73
bunting 77
buttons, sewing on 35

• C •
casings 52
changing stitch types 23
corners, sewing 21, 23
cotton twill tape 32

• D •
dish towels 46-57
apron 52-53
dust cover 54-55
shoe bag 56-57
tote bag 48-49
wrap'n'roll 50-51
dust cover 54-55

• F •
fabric 30-31
right side 31
wrong side 31
felt 30
floppy pots 98-101
flutterbys 74-75

• G •
garlands 96-97
goodie bags 58-59

• H •
hand sewing 34-35
buttons 35
stitches 35
handy bags 78-81
hook and loop tape 32

• I •
ironing 29, 37

• M •
make it easy pillows 60-67
muslin 30

• O •
opening out a seam, see ironing

• P •
pillows, make it easy 60-67
pinning 36
pin watch 94-95
playful pups 102-105
pom-poms 72
problem solving 24

• R •
raw edge 31
removing the fabric 23
reverse stitch 20, 23
right side, fabric 31
running stitch 35

• S •
scissors 28
pinking shears 29
seam allowance 37
seams 36-37
allowance 37
opening out 37

sewing 37
unpicking 37
selvage 31
sewing 18-21
changing stitch types 23
corners 21
hand position 18
hand sewing 34-35
reverse stitch 20, 23
seams 37
sitting position 18
starting 19
stopping 18-19
straight stitch 20
tips 24
sewing essentials 27-32
sewing kit 27
sewing machine 12-13
choosing 13
safety 13
shoe bag 56-57
sleep well, Ted
114-117
slip stitch 35
soft heart, make a 40-43
soft-toy filling 32
Square Peg and friends 82-93
straight stitch 20
tips 20-21
streamers
flutterbys 74-76

• T •
templates, making 38-39
tracing 39
threads 29
tips, sewing 24
tote bag 48-49
toys
3-D chickens 112-113
bobtail rabbits 68-73
monster invasion 118-121
playful pups 102-105

sleep well, Ted 114-117
Square Peg and friends
82-93
trims 32

• U •
unpicking a seam 37

• W •
wacky ornaments 106-107
whipstitch 25
wrap'n'roll 50-51
wrong side, fabric 31

• Z •
zip it! 108-111

Acknowledgments

Dorling Kindersley would like to thank:
Isabella and Maria Thomson for modeling; Anne Hildyard for proofreading;
Nicola Powling, Senior Jacket Creative and Francesca Young, Jacket Coordinator;
Charlotte Bull for her illustrations; and JJ Locations for location rental.